Blogs, Wikis, Podcasts,

THIRD EDITION

and Other Powerful **Web Tools** for Classrooms

Blogs, Wikis, Podcasts,

THIRD EDITION

and Other Powerful **Web Tools** for Classrooms

Will Richardson

CORWIN
A SAGE Company

For information:

Corwin
A SAGE Company
2455 Teller Road
Thousand Oaks, California 91320
(800) 233–9936
Fax: (800) 417–2466
www.corwin.com

SAGE India Pvt. Ltd.
B 1/I 1 Mohan Cooperative
    Industrial Area
Mathura Road, New Delhi 110 044
India

SAGE Ltd.
1 Oliver's Yard
55 City Road
London EC1Y 1SP
United Kingdom

SAGE Asia-Pacific Pte. Ltd.
33 Pekin Street #02-01
Far East Square
Singapore 048763

Printed in the United States of America

Library of Congress Cataloging-in-Publication Data

Richardson, Will.
Blogs, wikis, podcasts, and other powerful Web tools for classrooms/Will Richardson.—3rd ed.
    p. cm.
Includes bibliographical references and index.
ISBN 978-1-4129-7747-0 (pbk.)
    1. Internet in education. 2. Educational Web sites. 3. Teaching--Aids and devices.
I. Title.

LB1044.87.R53 2010
371.33′44678—dc22   2009051376

This book is printed on acid-free paper.

10   11   12   13   14   10   9   8   7   6   5   4   3   2

Acquisitions Editor:	Hudson Perigo
Associate Editor:	Julie McNall
Editorial Assistant:	Allison Scott
Production Editor:	Eric Garner
Copy Editor:	Nancy Conger
Typesetter:	C&M Digitals (P) Ltd.
Proofreader:	Joyce Li
Indexer:	Jean Casalegno
Cover Designer:	Rose Storey
Graphic Designer:	Anthony Paular

Contents

Preface to
the Third
Edition

It's been over four years since the first edition of this book was published
and now, over 50,000 copies later, it's feeling like the world is a bit of a
different place. Whereas blogs and RSS feeds and wikis were still just blips
on the radar back in 2006, today, social Web media and online networks are
a part of the mainstream conversation when it comes to politics, media, and
business. And, yes, to some extent, education. Not that schools are rushing to
embrace these tools in any systemic way . . . yet. However, there's no doubt
that more teachers, more administrators, more parents, and more students are
beginning to understand how learning is changing because of the connections we can make on the Web. That's the good news.

The not-so-good news is that those numbers are still nowhere near large
enough. Just like we did four years ago, we live in a world where the following condition still exists: A growing majority of students are immersed in
social networks and technologies outside of school, and most have no adults
in their lives who are teaching them how to use those connections to learn. At
a time when our access to information, people, and ideas is exploding online,
that reality is simply unacceptable. Our collective inability to recognize a
"tectonic shift" in the way we learn stems, I believe, from one fundamental
fact—not enough of us have experienced that shift for ourselves. These shifts
will not come under the guise of "twenty-first-century skills" reforms which
are actually nineteenth-century skills being remarketed for a new day. They
will only come when enough educators fully understand the open connections, open conversations, open content, and open learning that come as a part
of a community of learners who are invested in their own passions.

The tools that are discussed in this book are simply that: tools. And as
the chapters herein illustrate, learning how to use the tools is not difficult. If

you're looking for complex code, you won't find it here. But just because learning the tools is easy, learning *with* the tools is more nuanced. While each one of these technologies allow us to publish easily to the Web, simple publishing does not guarantee connection and network building. While a great many teachers have taken steps to use these tools to publish student work to the Web, far too often those pieces reflect work that we used to do with pen and paper simply published in a different way. None of the pedagogies have changed to reflect the fact that the real learning takes places *after* we publish, through the connections we make with others to extend the meaning of what we publish in new and profound ways. That's the real power of "The Read/Write Web."

And so, this remains the central message of this book: In order for us to prepare our students for what is without question a future filled with networked learning spaces, we must first experience those environments for ourselves. We must become connected and engaged in learning in these new ways if we are to fully understand the pedagogies of using these tools with our students. We cannot honestly discuss twenty-first-century learning skills for our students until we make sense of them for ourselves. So while this is a book about tools, I have made more of an effort to contextualize all of these technologies in ways that will help you grow your own connections, your own networks, and, in the process, your own learning. Read this book for yourself first, for your classroom second.

What continues to amaze me is the way my own learning deepens and evolves, due in large measure to my personal passion as a parent to understand these shifts for my own kids, and due also to the incredible people in my personal learning network who contribute so much to the conversation, push my thinking at every turn, and sustain me with their own passions for their students and classrooms. In particular, I'd like to acknowledge my friend and Powerful Learning Practice partner Sheryl Nussbaum-Beach whose infectious "change-the-world" attitude continually motivates my thinking and my work, and my friend Chris Lehmann, whose work as principal at the Science Leadership Academy in Philadelphia serves as a model for any educator seeking excellence in a fast-changing world. In addition, I'd like to thank the likes of Bruce Dixon, Alec Couros, David Jakes, Gary Stager, Sylvia Martinez, Dean Shareski, Karl Fisch, Bud Hunt, Clarence Fisher, John Pederson, George Siemens, Stephen Downes, Jay Rosen, Jeff Jarvis, Warren Buckleitner, Rob Mancabelli, and the hundreds of others of generous people who share their learning with me on a regular basis.

It's an amazing time to be a learner. My sincerest hope is that the ideas and examples captured here will bring you a sense of just how amazing this moment could be in your own learning life.

About the Author

Will Richardson is an internationally known "evangelist" for the use of Weblogs, RSS, and related Internet technologies in classrooms and schools. A former classroom teacher for more than 20 years, he integrated social Web technologies into his curriculum for over four years, and over the past four years has spoken to thousands of educators around the world on the merits of "The Read/Write Web." In various Weblog projects, his students collaborated with best-selling authors, Pulitzer Prize-winning journalists, and students in classrooms from around the globe. One of the first educator bloggers, his own Weblog at www.weblogg-ed.com has been featured in the *New York Times, Washington Times, Syllabus,* and others, and it is a primary resource for the creation and implementation of Weblog technologies on the K–12 level. His articles have appeared in *Educational Leadership, English Journal, Edutopia,* and *Principal Leadership,* among others, and he has presented and given workshops about Weblogs, RSS, and other technologies at national conventions such as the National Education Computing Conference (NECC), Association for Supervision and Curriculum Development (ASCD), Journalism Education Association, and many others. He also writes "The Online Edge" column for *District Administration Magazine* and is an adjunct instructor in the Seton Hall University Executive EdD program. In addition, he is a national advisory board member for the George Lucas Education Foundation.

Will is cofounder of Powerful Learning Practice (plpnetwork.com), which delivers long-term, job-embedded professional development to thousands of teachers around the world each year.

1 The Read/ Write Web

Tim Berners-Lee had a grand vision for the Internet when he began development of the World Wide Web in 1989. "The original thing I wanted to do," Berners-Lee says, "was make it a collaborative medium, a place where we [could] all meet and read and write" (as cited in Carvin, 2005). At the time, the Internet was not much more than a network of computers that researchers and government officials used to share text and data; it was just a small blip on the radar screens of all but the most technologically savvy. But Berners-Lee saw the potential to construct a vast "web" of linked information, built by people from around the globe, creating the ability to share not just data but personal talents and experiences in new and powerful ways.

The first part of Berners-Lee's dream came to fruition in 1993, with the development of the Mosaic Web browser. Seemingly overnight, the Internet went from a text- and numbers-based research tool for the few to a colorful, graphic world of information for the masses. Even though content was limited in those early days, millions of people soon started going online to read or "surf" the Web for information and entertainment. And as access spread, connections became faster, and more and more Web designers and authors set up shop, the twentieth century ended with the Internet taking its place as an essential communications and research network connecting people around the globe.

But even with that initial period of immense and rapid growth, the original vision of being able to read *and* write to the Web was slow (in Internet terms, at least) to be realized. Writing to the Web required knowledge of the HTML codes that make Web pages work and of the protocols to get those pages up and running. To be sure, there were text-based newsgroups to share ideas and some sites like Amazon.com where readers could leave reviews and opinions. But for the most part, the ability to create content on the Web was nowhere near as easy as consuming it, and even those who could create did so with little means for easy collaboration.

A NEW WORLD WIDE WEB

Today, however, this inability to create is no longer the case.

The past few years have seen the development of an explosion of easy Internet publishing tools that have done much to fulfill Berners-Lee's concept of a Read/Write Web. As early as 2003, a Pew Internet & American Life Project found that more than 53 million American adults, or 44 percent of adult Internet users, had used the Internet to publish their thoughts, respond to others, post pictures, share files, and otherwise contribute to the explosion of content available online (Lenhart, Fallows, & Horrigan, 2004). And in 2007, another Pew study showed that 64 percent of all teens who use the Internet could be considered "content creators" (Lenhart, Madden, Macgill, & Smith, 2007). Today, in 2010, those numbers have no doubt increased significantly.

In early 2009, Technorati.com, one of many blog-tracking services, listed over 133 million blogs (short for Weblogs). Blogs are the first widely adopted easy publishing tool of the Read/Write Web, which people use to create personal journals of their lives, build resource sites with colleagues, or filter the news of the day for audiences large and small with no need to know how to code pages or transfer files. And there is no doubt that blogs have become an influential medium in all walks of life, from politics to personal passions. Today, we are beginning to create and share our thoughts and lives online as a natural part of our daily lives. The Read/Write Web has arrived.

And it's not just blogs. In the last few years, multimedia publishing by the masses has exploded. In early 2009, over 20 hours' worth of videos were being uploaded to YouTube.com each minute (that's right, I said minute), and YouTube.com is just one of dozens of popular video-publishing sites on the Web. Millions of photos, thousands of audio files, and countless other creations are now being added every day to the incredibly vast storehouse of information that the Web has become. As more people get more access to broadband connections and more powerful computers and even easier tools, this trend shows every sign of continuing to grow. We're in the midst of an explosion of technologies that will continue to remake the Web into the community-driven, participatory space Berners-Lee originally envisioned, changing our lives in many significant ways. These changes are already playing out in politics, journalism, and business. And from an educational standpoint, this new Read/Write Web promises to transform much of how we teach and learn as well.

For most, however, even now, over a decade into the Read/Write Web, the significance of these changes is still just starting to be realized. We are no longer limited to being independent readers or consumers of information; as we'll see, we can also be collaborators in the creation of large storehouses of information. In the process, we can learn much about our world and ourselves. In almost every area of life, the Read/Write Web is changing our relationship to technology and rewriting the age-old paradigms of how things work. No doubt, these changes will take many more years to process. In fact, what author Dan Gillmor wrote a few years ago still holds true today: "The people who'll understand this best are probably just being born" (Gillmor, 2005).

EXTRAORDINARY CHANGES

Clay Shirky, the author of *Here Comes Everybody: The Power of Organizing Without Organizations*, writes that these new Web technologies are creating a "tectonic shift" in the world, not simply because of what they allow us to publish, but because of what happens after we publish. Simply put, when we share online, we create the potential for connections in ways that were simply not possible even a few years ago. And in the context of those connections, we can form groups around our various passions and interests, a capability that fundamentally changes almost everything.

> Anything that changes the way groups get things done will affect society as a whole. . . . For any given organization, the important questions are "When will the change happen?" and "What will change?" The only two answers we can rule out are never, and nothing. The ways in which any given institution will find its situation transformed will vary, but the various local changes are manifestations of a single deep source: newly capable groups are assembling, and they are working without the managerial imperative and outside the previous strictures that bounded their effectiveness. These changes will transform the world everywhere groups of people come together to accomplish something, which is to say everywhere. (Shirky, 2008, p. 3)

No question, the Read/Write Web holds transformational changes in store for teachers and students of all stripes. We will not be immune to these shifts. But, as is often the case, education has been slow to adapt to these new tools and potentials. In other areas of our lives, however, we can see some of these transformations happening right now, right in front of our eyes.

Take politics, for example. No question that one of the main reasons for the success of the Obama campaign in 2008 was its understanding of the potentials inherent in the group-forming ability we now have. On his MyBarackObama.com site, supporters formed over 27,000 groups, everything from "Bartenders for Barack" (21 members) to "Ravelry Knitters for Obama" (343 members), and within those groups they raised money, held rallies, and got out the vote. Both his MySpace and Facebook pages had over 1 million "friends" and President Obama's Twitter feed currently has over 1.7 million followers. (We'll go over Twitter in detail in Chapter 6.) There is no debate any longer that politicians who aren't taking advantage of the connective tissue of these technologies are putting themselves at risk of irrelevance.

The ability to easily publish text, pictures, and video is also changing the face of journalism and media as we know it. There is no better example than the coverage of last year's uprising in Iran after the contested elections in June. Despite the best attempts of the government to crack down on traditional reporters in terms of getting news out of the country, tens of thousands of Iranian citizen journalists armed with cell phone and computers captured the attention of the world with their nonstop photos, videos, blog posts, and Tweets. While long-standing media outlets like the *New York Times* and National Public Radio did their best to filter, edit, and synthesize all of the information coming out of the protests, those of us interested in learning more could access the raw accounts on YouTube.com or on Flickr.com (a photo-sharing site), much of it being distributed through channels that didn't even exist a year or two ago. And, as with the heartbreaking Indian Ocean earthquake and resulting tsunami in 2004, and the horrible devastation caused by Hurricane Katrina in New Orleans in 2005, one of the best places to get the latest information about what was occurring in Iran was at Wikipedia. In the first week of protests, the article on the "2009 Iranian Election Protests" was updated almost 2,000 times by hundreds of contributors who left over 145 citations at the bottom of the page. In essence, it became a clearinghouse of information based on the work of amateur researchers who published facts and photos and links as they found them. We're seeing a new model of journalism evolving right in front of us, one that is much more immediate and much more complex in terms of who to trust and what to believe. And that new model has been repeated over and over as big news stories hit on national or local levels.

In reality, the Read/Write Web has created millions of amateur reporters who now have their own digital printing presses. It's also created millions of amateur editors who are, in blogging parlance, ready to "fact-check your a**" whenever a major story breaks. And today, even the newspapers themselves are inviting their readers to participate, understanding what former reporter turned blogger Dan Gillmor knew early on: "If my readers know more than I do (which I know they do), I can include them in the process of making my journalism better" (as cited in Koman, 2005). In 2007, *USA TODAY* was among the first to make it possible for readers to comment on any story—adding opinions, asking further questions, or even correcting what was written—and most other online newspapers have since followed suit. In essence, every article is a blog post. By including people in the process, this new Web creates all sorts of opportunities for participatory journalism, which, of course, creates all sorts of new definitions and descriptions of just what journalism is. Traditional media outlets such as *The Washington Post,* the BBC, and others, are scrambling to respond to this trend, creating interactive spaces for readers, buying on-the-spot news photos from people with camera phones, and running amateur video of news events. These are huge, transformative shifts to a model that has lasted for hundreds of years, and these changes show no signs of slowing.

More recently, businesses have begun exploring the use of Weblogs, wikis, and even Twitter for a variety purposes, from public relations to customer service to internal communications. When Microsoft began offering up Weblog space to some of its developers a few years ago, potential customers had an opportunity not only to read about the inner workings of the company, but they also had a chance to respond and participate. And IBM, one of the most successful companies in history, is transforming the way it connects and communicates. As of mid-2007, IBM was running over 20,000 internal wiki sites, 26,000 blogs, and over 400,000 of its full- and part-time employees were participating in "Blue Pages," IBM's own MySpace-type social networking system. This new transparency and opening up is now an expectation, especially in a world where users of particular products can connect and communicate their experiences with one another. In this world, we create our own advertisements, and businesses have to play by some very different rules. Now, hundreds of corporations including GM, Coca-Cola, Sun Microsystems, and Apple have blogs and wikis, and many CEOs are beginning to catch on to blogging as well.

No matter how you look at it, we are creating what author Douglas Rushkoff calls a "society of authorship" where every teacher and every student—every person with access—will have the ability to contribute ideas and experiences to the larger body of knowledge that is the Internet. And in doing so, Rushkoff says, we will be writing the human story, in real time, together—a vision that asks each of us to participate (Rushkoff, 2004).

In addition, this new Web is forcing us to reexamine many of the basic ways in which we live our lives. These technologies make more of our lives transparent to others in ways that many find unsettling. There is also a growing gap between how this digital generation defines privacy and the way most adults do. To our kids, making their lives come alive online is a part of the way they live. Communicating and collaborating with peers using instant or text messaging, Twitter or their MySpace, accounts allows them to be "always on" and always connected. That is their expectation, one that has changed greatly in just the past ten years. And the reality is that we are not going to get any less plugged in or any less open in terms of how we live our lives. These shifts will only become more acute.

THE READ/WRITE WEB IN EDUCATION

For all these reasons and more, I think this is a hugely challenging time to be an educator. The world is changing around us, yet as a system, we have been very, very slow to react. Our students' realities in terms of the way they communicate and learn are very different from our own. By and large, they are "out there" using a wide variety of technologies that they are told they can't use when they come to school. They are building vast social networks with little or no guidance from adults. They are using much more complex and flexible digital information with hardly any instruction on how it differs from the paper world.

In the four years since the first printing of this book, tens of thousands of teachers and students have begun using some of these tools, but the vast majority of educators still have little or no context for these shifts. And, more importantly, very few people, educators or otherwise, have yet to experience the transformative potential of these new tools in terms of their own personal learning. Without question, our ability to easily publish content online and to connect to vast networks of passionate learners will force us to rethink the way we communicate with our constituents, the way we deliver our curriculum, and the expectations we have of our students. The Web also has the potential to radically change what we assume about teaching and learning, and it presents us with important questions to consider: What needs to change about our curriculum when our students have the ability to reach audiences far beyond our classroom walls? What changes must we make in our teaching as it becomes easier to bring primary sources to our students? How do we need to rethink our ideas of literacy when we must prepare our students to become not only readers and writers, but editors and collaborators and publishers as well? And, I think most importantly, how can we as learners begin to take advantage of the opportunities these tools present, so we may understand more clearly the pedagogies used in the classroom? At its heart, the implications of this new Web are all about learning first, teaching second.

On first blush, these new technologies may not seem well suited to a climate of standardized test scores and government accountability. Some see the constructionist, collaborative pedagogy of Weblogs, wikis, digital photo and video, and others as presenting a risk instead of a solution for a system whose students continue to struggle to stay apace of their international peers. In reality, however, these tools have considerable relevance to state and local core content curriculum standards, and there is much reason to believe their implementation in schools will better prepare students for a slew of new literacies and competencies in their post-education lives.

SOCIAL LEARNING

Today's schools are faced with a difficult dilemma that pits a student body that has grown up immersed in technology against a teaching faculty that is less agile with the tools of the trade. The National Technology Plan released in January 2005 went so far as to admit that "today's students, of almost any age, are far ahead of their teachers in computer literacy. They prefer to access subject information on the Internet, where it is more abundant, more accessible, and more up-to-date" (National Educational Technology Plan, 2005). And a survey in 2008 by the Pew Internet & American Life Project estimated that over 65 percent of adolescents had a MySpace or a Facebook account, a number that far outpaces the use of such sites by educators. And even the youngest in our midst—kids in second, third, and fourth grade—are migrating to sites like Club Penguin and Webkinz, social networking sites with training wheels. There is no question that more and more of today's kids are entering our classrooms having had years of "screen time" and that in general, while they still may have a lot to learn about living in the digital world, they are by and large fearless in their use of technology.

Take, for example, 13-year-old Matthew Bischoff, who in 2004 became a "podcasting" sensation by creating "Escape From the World," a regular digital broadcast of technology-related news that he produced and posted to the Web from his bedroom (www.matthewbischoff.com). Or 18-year-old Sam Jackson, whose blog chronicling his college admissions process became a highly visited resource for thousands of high schoolers (www.samjackson.org/college). Or my 12-year-old daughter Tess, whose "Weather Recipes" book, which we scanned and uploaded to Flickr.com when she was eight, has been viewed almost 3,400 times as of this writing (only 50 or so by me, I swear: tinyurl.com/2nfw64/). All around us, kids are creating content in ways that most adults haven't yet tried.

Results of a Netday survey released in March 2005 assert that technology has become "an indispensable tool in the education of today's students." The survey showed that 81 percent of students in Grades 7–12 have e-mail accounts, 75 percent have at least one Instant Messenger (IM) screen name, and that 97 percent believe strongly that technology use is important in education. And, the fastest-growing age group for using the Internet is 2 to 5 year olds (NetDay News, 2005). According to author and technologist Marc Prensky, "this online life is a whole lot bigger than just the Internet. This online life has become an entire strategy for how to live, survive, and thrive in the twenty-first century where cyberspace is a part of everyday life" (Prensky, 2004).

This immersion in technology has neurological effects as well. William D. Winn, director of the Learning Center at the University of Washington, believes that years of computer use results in children who "think differently from us. They develop hypertext minds. They leap around. It's as though their cognitive structures were parallel, not sequential" (Prensky, 2001a). In other words, today's students may not be well suited to the more linear progression of learning that most educational systems employ. Most teachers in today's schools, meanwhile, were not surrounded by technology growing up. And the speed with which these technologies have been developed (remember, the Web browser is only 15 years old) means that it's a daunting task for many to catch up to their students.

The bad news is that the Read/Write Web threatens to make these differences between teachers and learners even more acute. Whereas students are open to the ways of new technologies, schools by and large are not. Howard Rheingold, author of *Smart Mobs,* says "The kind of questioning, collaborative, active, lateral rather than hierarchical pedagogy that participatory media both forces and enables is not the kind of change that takes place quickly or at all in public schools" (Rheingold, 2007, p. 2). All of this paints the picture of an educational system that is out of touch with the way its students learn.

The good news, however, is that the tools discussed in this book have just as much chance of closing this gap as widening it. The reason is because by their very nature, they are relatively easy for anyone to employ in the classroom. The sudden explosion in online content creation could not occur if technological barriers to entry were high, and these barriers will continue to come down as the tools themselves continue to evolve. Even more important is that most of the tools of the Read/Write Web are free and will most likely stay that way as open-source software alternatives continue to grow. That doesn't mean that it won't be work for many teachers to get up to speed with these new tools and teaching methods. But on the whole, we can be optimistic that once the potential of the Read/Write Web finds its way into schools, students and teachers will be launched on a path of discovery and learning like they have never experienced before.

LEARNERS AS TEACHERS

As you read this book, I have one request: Before you attempt to bring these technologies to your students, first be selfish about their use in your own learning practice. While there is no doubt my classes were in many ways profoundly changed by blogs ,wikis, and the like, the bigger truth is that the transformation in my own personal learning practice is what informed my work with students. It wasn't until I fully understood how these technologies could facilitate global connections and conversations around my own passions, and how they could help me create powerful learning networks and communities, that I was able to see what needed to change in terms of my curriculum and my teaching.

Learning in this environment is about being able to construct, develop, sustain, and participate in global networks that render time and place less and less relevant. In fact, in a world where our students will hold between 12 and 14 jobs by the time they reach 38 years old, it's imperative we develop in them a kind of network literacy to guide them in this process.

That doesn't mean that every teacher needs to start a blog or create a wiki or a podcast. But it does mean that, as educators, we must tap into the potentials that these tools give us for learning. And that doesn't just mean learning about our craft or technology or our curriculum. It means learning about whatever we are passionate about. For me, that's figuring out how these shifts and how these tools change the nature of learning and what that implies for education. But it also means learning more about the Chicago Cubs, photography, and many other topics that hold my interest. For you, it can mean a whole array of different things.

The common thread, I believe, is that we make these connections in our own practice first so we can thoroughly understand the pedagogical implications for the classroom. Since the first edition of this book went to press in 2006, tens of thousands of teachers and students have begun to implement these technologies. But the reality is that the vast majority of educators have taken the work they had students do in the paper, analog world and simply digitized it. And I think that's because they haven't experienced the connections that come after the work is published and shared. Giving students a chance to share their work with a global audience is an important first step, but there is much more to it. It's the conversations, the links, and the networks that grow from them afterward that really show us the profound implications for lifelong learning.

So, as you read and consider these tools, I would urge you to ask yourselves the following questions:

- What are your passions?
- Who are your teachers? Are they all in physical space?
- How are you building your own learning networks using these tools?
- In this new environment, how are you modeling your learning for your students?

THE TOOLBOX

Just what are the technologies that are changing the way we teach and learn? It seems the number grows each day, but the teacher's toolbox that will be covered in this book is made up of a mix of those that publish, those that manage information, and those that share content in new collaborative ways. This toolbox contains the following items:

1. *Weblogs*. Thousands of teachers and students have already incorporated Weblogs into their classrooms and into their practice. Blogs, as they are known, are easily created, easily updateable Web sites that allow an author (or authors) to publish instantly to the Internet from any Internet connection. They can also be interactive, allowing teachers and students to begin conversations or add to the information published there. Weblogs are the most widely adopted tool of the Read/Write Web so far.

2. *Wikis*. A wiki is a collaborative Web space where anyone can add content and anyone can edit content that has already been published. In schools, teachers and students have begun using password-protected wikis to create their own textbooks and resource sites.

3. *Really Simple Syndication (RSS)*. RSS is a technology that allows educators to subscribe to "feeds" of the content that is created on the Internet, whether it's written in a Weblog or in a more traditional space such as a newspaper or magazine. In other words, just as in traditional models of syndication, content comes to the reader instead of the reader retrieving the content. From a research and information management standpoint, RSS may be the new "killer app" (extremely useful application) for education.

4. *Aggregators*. An aggregator collects and organizes the content generated via the RSS feed.

5. *Social Bookmarking*. Bookmarking sites allow users to do more than just save the Web addresses of interesting content. They allow readers to save and archive entire pages, thus producing a form of a searchable, "personal Internet." In addition, social bookmarking sites like Diigo.com and Delicious.com allow teachers and students to build subject-specific resource lists that they can easily share when using RSS. This in turn creates a community of information gatherers who extend the reach of any one person.

6. *Online Photo Galleries*. Publishing digital photos to the Web not only means sharing pictures with family and friends, it means becoming a part of a community of photographers sharing ideas and experiences. And, as we'll see, it means adding another dimension to what teachers and students can do with digital images in the classroom.

7. *Audio/Video Casting.* New technologies make it easy to not only produce digital voice and video files, they also make it easy to publish and distribute them to wide Internet audiences. Students can now easily "write" in many different media, a fact that opens up all sorts of possibilities for the classroom. They can also begin to create live streaming TV online.

8. *Twitter.* While Twitter has become all the rage for movie stars and millions of ordinary folks, it has also quietly become one of the most powerful tools for connecting and sharing the great content and professional development opportunities that are available to educators today.

9. *Social Networking Sites.* More and more schools are beginning to use out-of-the-box social networking sites like Ning.com and, dare I say it, Facebook, to help teach their students the network literacies that are required to navigate these new connections.

Although this list is not exhaustive, it is a relevant sampling of the types of tools being developed and the nature of their impact.

In and of itself, the "old" read-only Web was a transformative technology. It changed the way we work, the way we learn, and the way we communicate. I would argue that historians might look back on the first ten years of the Web the same way we look back on the early days of the printing press, the steam engine, or the automobile. The Web has changed our lives.

This "new" Read/Write Web will change it even more. As the former CEO of Hewlett-Packard, Carly Fiorina, said, the past 25 years in technology have been "the warm-up act." What we're entering is the "main event, and by main event I mean an era in which technology will truly transform every aspect of business, of government, of society, of life" (as cited in Friedman, 2005, p. 216). And, I would add, education.

This book will focus on the ways these technologies can help educators take full advantage of the potentials for personal learning with the new Web and show ways in which teachers can effectively bring these technologies to their students to enhance their learning and better prepare them for their post-education worlds. Throughout, we will discuss the pedagogies and literacies that surround successful implementation of the tools in the classroom.

KEEPING STUDENTS SAFE

Before launching headfirst into a discussion of the tools, it's important to take some time to talk about keeping our students safe on the Read/Write

Web. Obviously, this is about more than not publishing children's names and pictures on the Internet or permitting students to access obscene content online—acts that federal and state laws already regulate. Safety is now about responsibility, appropriateness, and common sense as well. If we ask our students to publish, even if we know they are publishing outside of the classroom (which they are), it's our obligation to teach them what is acceptable and safe and what isn't.

Like just about everything else in life, using the Web carries with it some risks. But again, like most other things, those risks can be greatly reduced by having the appropriate information in hand and by planning. Although cases of Internet predators are usually widely reported and are heart wrenching in nature, the actual numbers of Web-related abductions or seductions are very small. (See tinyurl.com/7fc819 for example.) That should not in any way minimize, however, our efforts to provide students with the knowledge they need to keep themselves safe.

Let's start with simply interacting with the Web. We all know that there is an overwhelming amount of inappropriate content on the Internet, be it pornography, bad language, or just bad taste. Schools and libraries are required by the Child Internet Protection Act (CIPA) to filter content that is accessible via the Internet. In addition, CIPA requires that schools monitor the online activities of minors and have a policy in place that addresses the "safety and security" of minors when online (FCC Consumer and Governmental Affairs Bureau, 2003). But as much as we may try to stop all forms of inappropriate content from being accessible from school, the reality is that some is not filtered.

It's not hard to imagine that along with more people being able to create and publish content to the Web will come more inappropriate content. Internet filters will become increasingly hard pressed to restrict such content. For example, there are thousands of obscure Weblogs that publish questionable content that falls outside the scope of the major filtering programs. I know—I've had the misfortune of running across some of them in my travels, and my students did as well. To deal with this, schools are faced with a couple of options. First, districts can choose to block some of the large Weblog hosting sites like Blogspot.com, Xanga.com, or MySpace.com. This eliminates millions of sites from student access and blocks not only the questionable sites but the large majority of perfectly appropriate sites that might be relevant to learning. I know of many bloggers, for instance, who write inspiringly and educationally about their work and their areas of expertise on their blogspot.com sites, sites that some schools have chosen to block.

The other alternative, of course, is to teach students the skills they need to navigate the darker sides of the Web safely and effectively. I remember back in the days before CIPA when our classroom access to the Web was unfiltered. My students and I spent a good deal of time talking about how responsible use meant not just refraining from actively seeking out these inappropriate sites, but also reacting appropriately when they were happened upon. I'll never forget the day I was sitting in between two students as they were working on the Web when suddenly one of them let out an audible gasp. He had been researching tattoos, and when I turned to see what was on his screen, I gasped almost as loudly. (Use your imagination.) But my student reacted the way he should have; he quickly hit the back button on the browser and without making a big deal about it went about his work. Later, as a class, we talked about the incident and reinforced the proper reaction the student had. My students knew that they could not be kept totally safe from the ne'er-do-wells of the world, but they also knew they had a choice as to how they responded when faced with such a situation.

Teachers working with younger children obviously have more to be concerned about, and I would urge a great deal of planning and testing before going online. Create your own Web tours beforehand and limit the amount of freedom students have to surf. But even in the early grades, teaching appropriate use is critical. Kids are coming to the Web earlier and earlier, and it's obviously very important that we prepare them for life online. And we should take every opportunity to model appropriate use in our own practice, even with the youngest kids. They need to see us using the Web and leveraging the information there for our own learning, even if they are too young to fully understand the potential for themselves.

From a content-creation and publishing standpoint, there are other issues to deal with. The first, of course, is protecting the privacy of students. Let's start with personal information. Most states now have laws that require parents to decide how much personal information about their children may be published on the school Web site. Parents in my state, New Jersey, may opt to allow photos, full names, and even addresses to be published to the site. So, the first step for any teacher thinking about having students publish online is to make sure to get parental approval. The best way to do this is to send a letter home to parents clearly explaining your plans and asking permission for students to participate. That letter should include a description of the technology, how it will be used, what security measures have been put in place, what your expectations are for your students, and what the curricular goals are for its use. (See the example of a letter dealing with the use of blogs at the end of this chapter.) It would also be well advised to discuss your use of blogs with supervisors and administrators as well.

From a student standpoint, teachers have to be ready to discuss what should and should not be published online. Obviously, students should never reveal information about where they live, where they work, and anything else that might identify them to potential predators. This, in fact, is one of the biggest issues with personal journal sites like MySpace and Facebook. Many adolescents who use these sites include full names, addresses, and provocative pictures of themselves—behavior that can only increase their chances of getting into trouble. In addition, students need to know that any content they create online will become a part of their Web portfolio. They need to ask themselves, "What if someone finds this piece five or ten years from now?"

One of the most difficult roads to navigate in the world of the Read/Write Web is how to balance the safety of the child with the benefits that come with students taking ownership of the work they publish online. First, we need to decide who the audience is. Is it just a small peer group? The whole class? The entire Internet? As we'll see, there are ways to set the size and shape of the intended audience for what our students create. Then, we need to think about how clearly to identify who the student is. Complete anonymity is the safest route when publishing, no doubt, but it detracts from the personal achievement and ownership that a student feels in publishing her work. Using a full name can help in that regard, but it adds a layer of risk to the process. On the K–12 level at least, most teachers take the middle ground by having students use just first names when publishing. Some, however, do give the option of using a pseudonym for students who may have unique first names. Others opt for complete anonymity by assigning a number to each student to use. Either way, it's an important balance for teachers, students, and parents to negotiate.

Because most of these tools are collaborative and offer the potential to work with other students or mentors or primary sources outside of school, teachers need to think about ways to vet the people who are allowed into the process. With blogs, for instance, the ability for people to leave comments can be a very powerful and positive learning tool. If, however, there is unchecked access to commenting on a student site, it may open up the door to inappropriate or irrelevant feedback. Again, this is something my students and I would talk about. What happens if someone we don't know leaves a comment? What if the comment is distasteful? In my experience, the vast majority of instances in which outsiders commented on student work were positive. But teachers and districts need to find their own balance.

Today, despite the relative newness of these tools, thousands of teachers and students are using Weblogs, wikis, RSS, and the rest to enhance student learning in safe, productive, effective ways. No doubt, employing these tools is not as simple as exchanging paper in a closed classroom environment. But the learning opportunities that these tools offer makes it worth all of our whiles to create best practices in our own right.

SAMPLE BLOGGING LETTER FROM TINYURL.COM/636VH5

Dear Families:

From now to the end of the year, Ms. Tammy's class will be taking part in a pilot writing program designed to help them develop their writing and explore their interests by sharing their writing with a real audience. Students will be using personal Weblogs to post their writing to the Internet.

A Weblog, or blog as it is commonly called, is a special type of Web page that can be created and easily updated using a Web browser. Each new entry has its own date stamp. Each entry has a comments section where visitors to the blog may leave comments for the author.

How It Works

Each week Ms. Tammy will teach a writing lesson using the six-trait writing model. After the lesson, students will write an entry for their blog. They may choose the topic, but they need to make use of the skills taught in the lesson to help craft their writing. The emphasis is on the quality, not the quantity of what they write. When students are done polishing their writing, they have it reviewed by a teacher before it is published to the Web.

Students will have two extra computer sessions most weeks to provide them with the time needed to complete their weekly blogging assignment. Students may also work from home. All that is required is an Internet connection and a Web browser. Students are able to save their work as drafts before publishing it to their blog. Directions for working from home will be provided.

Having a real audience is one of the key components to this program. In addition to receiving comments from their classmates, Ms. Tammy's students will receive comments from other fourth- and fifth-grade classes who visit their blogs. We are arranging for students in other parts of the world to visit our blogs and comment on the writing. Parents are also invited to visit the blogs and respond to the writing. Potentially, anyone on the Internet could respond to our blogs, however, it is not likely that the world at large will stumble across them.

Security

This blogging project is designed to minimize risk to your child. The only personally identifying information included in the blog will be their first name. There will be no mention of our school name or our location. Students are allowed to post their interests and opinions, but not their age, e-mail address, photographs of themselves, or other sensitive information.

Assessment

The weekly blog assignments will be part of your child's language arts grade this term. As with other projects they have completed this year, students will receive a scoring rubric that explains the expectations for these assignments. The rubric will include a section for the comments they leave in other students' blogs.

(Continued)

(Continued)

Resources

- Blogs created by fifth-grade students in the USA (tinyurl.com/31v436)
- BBC News article about blogging in a school in the UK (tinyurl.com/35g9q)

Permission

Before your child may start posting to their blog, we are asking for you and your child to discuss and sign the following form. Please return the form to Ms. Tammy.

Blogging Terms and Conditions

1. Students using blogs are expected to act safely by keeping personal information out of their posts. You agree not to post or give out your family name, password, username, e-mail address, home address, school name, city, country, or other information that could help someone locate or contact you in person. You may share your interests, ideas, and preferences.

2. Students using blogs agree not to share their username or password with anyone besides their teachers and parents. You agree to never log in as another student.

3. Students using blogs are expected to treat blog spaces as classroom spaces. Speech that is inappropriate for class is not appropriate for your blog. While we encourage you to engage in debate and conversation with other bloggers, we also expect that you will conduct yourself in a manner reflective of a representative of this school.

4. Student blogs are to be a forum for student expression. However, they are first and foremost a tool for learning, and as such will sometimes be constrained by the various requirements and rules of classroom teachers. Students are welcome to post on any school-appropriate subject.

5. Students blogs are to be a vehicle for sharing student writing with real audiences. Most visitors to your blog who leave comments will leave respectful, helpful messages. If you receive a comment that makes you feel uncomfortable or is not respectful, tell your teacher right away. Do not respond to the comment.

6. Students using blogs take good care of the computers by not downloading or installing any software without permission, and not clicking on ads or competitions.

7. Students who do not abide by these terms and conditions may lose their opportunity to take part in this project.

I have read and understood these blogging terms and conditions. I agree to uphold them.

Student's signature: _____ Date: _____

Parent's signature: _____ Date: _____

SOURCE: Used with permission of Susan Sedro.

2 Weblogs

Pedagogy and Practice

The first time I saw a Weblog, I knew I was looking at something very different from a "regular" Web page. Metafilter.org was one of only a handful of collaborative/community blogs back in 2001, where thousands of "members" were able to post funny or interesting links to a page, and where other members could leave their own opinions about those links just as easily. It was, and is, a fairly undistinguished looking site; lots of text and very few of the typical bells and whistles. But I will never forget the first time I posted my opinion, and the first time someone responded to it. There was something really powerful about so easily being able to share resources and ideas with a Web audience that was willing to share back what they thought about those ideas.

In essence, that's still what I find so powerful about Weblogs today, more than nine years later. Writing to the Web is easy. And there is an audience for my ideas. Those two concepts are at the core of why I think Weblogs have such huge potential in an educational setting.

What exactly is a Weblog? In its most general sense, a Weblog is an easily created, easily updateable Web site that allows an author (or authors) to publish instantly to the Internet from any Internet connection. The earliest blogs were literally "Web logs," or lists of sites a particular author visited on any given day that would be revised by changing the HTML code and updating the file on a server. But soon, the Internet geeks who maintained these sites developed software to automate the process and allow other people to collaborate. Happily, blogging today doesn't require any knowledge of code or FTP. It takes as much skill as sending an e-mail.

But what really distinguishes a blog from your run-of-the-mill Web site is much more than process; it's what you'll find there. Weblogs are not built on static chunks of content. Instead, they are comprised of reflections and conversations that in many cases are updated every day (if not three or four times a day). Blogs engage readers with ideas and questions and links. They ask readers to think and to respond. They demand interaction.

Take educator and blogger Dean Shareski's "Ideas and Thoughts" blog as an example (ideasandthoughts.org, as shown in Figure 2.1). Visitors to his site can see his latest post at the top of the left-hand column, and if they scroll down the page, they can read what Dean has been posting for the last couple of months. Among the things readers might find are reflections from his daily work, links to interesting or educational sites on the Web, ideas for lessons, and responses to the thoughts and ideas of other bloggers. And for every post, readers can leave comments that subsequent visitors to the site will be able to view. Typical comments on Dean's blog come from other teachers who share their own experiences, ask questions for clarification or to push his thinking, and offer links to other relevant pieces of content. In this way, blogs are a collaborative space, as readers become a part of the writing and learning process.

Dean Shareski's "Ideas and Thoughts" is one of many popular "edu" blogs. Like most, regular posts are featured in the left-hand column, while links to archives and other resources can be found in the side column. Dean's Weblog is also filled with links—another key characteristic of blogs. He has links to bookmarks that he's saved, personal affiliations, and archives of all

Figure 2.1 Dean Shareski's blog is one of the most widely read education blogs.

of his posts. Just about every post in his blog has a link in it, which is part of a good blog practice. (Being able to connect ideas and resources via linking is one of blogging's most important strengths.) And every post is itself a link so that others who read Dean's ideas can write about them on their own blogs and send their own readers Dean's way. That, in fact, is one of the key ways that community among bloggers is built.

But make no mistake, Dean's blog is every bit a Web site. He can include graphics, photos, video, and audio files; his blog can have almost any feature a more traditional Web site can have. Some of this depends upon the blog software and the skill level of the user, but for the most part, there isn't much that you can't do. And the best part is that most "blogwares" now come with a pretty impressive list of professional-looking templates right out the box, so even though Dean may have personalized the look of his site somewhat, there's no startup design even necessary.

Or take "Meredith's Page!" which was the name of the Weblog used by one of my former journalism students (tinyurl.com/42jzz7). Readers of her site will find reflections on the work she did in class, homework assignments handed in through the Weblog, and links to articles that she found relevant or interesting to her studies. She also has a running news feed from Google news about the topic she was writing her story about, teen apathy. In this way, she can easily check her blog to see if there are any new angles to her story. Readers will also find comments from classmates, teachers, and from Scott Higham, the Pulitzer Prize–winning journalist from the *Washington Post* who mentored her through her article process. Ultimately, Meredith's Weblog became her online archive of all the work related to our class.

In large measure, it is blogs that have opened up the Read/Write frontier for content creation to the Web, and over 180 million people have now taken advantage of the opportunity. Remember, two new blogs are being created every second, and that pace shows no sign of slowing down. Now, that doesn't mean that everyone who creates a blog becomes a dedicated blogger; two-thirds of all blogs go for more than two months without being updated. But it does mean that instant Web publishing for the masses is here. What those masses decide to do with it is another question. There are blogs about dogs and frogs, even people who wear clogs. There are flying blogs and frying blogs, crying blogs and dying blogs. There are blogs for every age (my 10-year-old son Tucker blogs), every occupation, every nationality, every . . . well, you get the idea. For some people, blogs are an important entry into the global conversation.

But just to be clear, there are, I think, variations on the blogging theme that are important to identify. Millions of young adults have created sites at Weblog hosting services like Facebook.com, MySpace.com, and Beebo.com, and by and large these authors are said to be bloggers. It's encouraging, to say the least, that so many of our would-be students have embraced the concept of publishing to the Web, and it bodes well for our use of these technologies in the classroom. What's somewhat discouraging, to me at least, is that these teenagers use these sites more as social tools than learning tools, and their behavior is sometimes reckless. There are continuing stories in the media heralding the dangers of blogs as resources for predators, and about teenagers divulging too much of themselves (in text and photo) online. Although that is definitely cause for concern and action, my fear is that the powerful instructional uses of the tool are being at best ignored and at worst not even considered. I would argue that what most adolescents are doing at these sites is more journaling than blogging, and from a classroom viewpoint, it's an important distinction to make. As I'll show a bit later, blogging is a genre that engages students and adults in a process of thinking in words, not simply an accounting of the day's events or feelings. In fact, learning specialists Fernette and Brock Eide's research shows that blogging in its truest form has a great deal of potentially positive impact on students. They found that blogs can

- promote critical and analytical thinking;
- be a powerful promoter of creative, intuitive, and associational thinking;
- promote analogical thinking;
- be a powerful medium for increasing access and exposure to quality information;
- combine the best of solitary reflection and social interaction (Eide Neurolearning Blog, 2005)

More about that later.

WEBLOGS IN SCHOOLS

Adopters of Weblogs in the classroom have already created a wide variety of ways to use them, and they have shown that blogs can enhance and deepen learning. Even at this still fairly early stage of development, blogs are being used as class portals, online filing cabinets for student work, e-portfolios, collaborative space, knowledge management, and even school Web sites. Through the unique process of blogging, which will be discussed in much more detail shortly, students are learning to read more critically, think about that reading more analytically, and write more clearly. And, they are building relationships with peers, teachers, mentors, and professionals within the Weblog environment.

If you're wondering just how flexible a Weblog can be as a teaching tool, see the lengthy list of uses created by Anne Davis, an elementary school teacher and Weblog advocate in Conyers, Georgia, at the end of this chapter. And with a little thought and experimentation, I'm sure we could add plenty more ideas as well. In the meantime, here's a closer look at how educators have been using Weblogs in their schools.

Class Portal

One trend that shows no sign of stopping is the movement of curriculum to a digital, online environment. Although some schools invest in expensive content management systems like Blackboard, many Weblog packages can accomplish almost as much at a much lesser cost. In this vein, a great entry point for Weblog use is to build a class portal to communicate information about the class and to archive course materials. From a teaching standpoint, having a place to publish the course curriculum, syllabus, class rules, home-work assignments, rubrics, handouts, and presentations makes a Weblog a powerful course management tool. When I created a portal for my journal-ism classes (see Figure 2.2), I was amazed at how frequently my students started using it and how much time I saved by not having to dig out duplicate copies of things that I had already handed out. Further, it drastically reduced the frequency of the "I didn't know we had homework" or "That was due today?" responses when my students didn't do their work. I'd just simply say, "It was on the blog."

Figure 2.2 A Class Portal Weblog

For the most part, parents love the transparency and the ability to access class materials. Most blogging software programs have automatic notification features, so parents can be notified when new information about the class is posted. (This could also be done via RSS, which we'll discuss in Chapter 5.)

The class portal Weblog makes it easy to communicate with peers who might be teaching the same course. I know my department chair liked the ability to visit the blog to see what we were up to and to get any information she might need about the class. Portals are a great way to get comfortable with the transparency that Weblogs provide.

Online Filing Cabinet

Giving students their own Weblogs can change much about the traditional classroom. Coupled with a classroom portal space, there's a good chance the class can go paperless as students simply post their work online for peer and teacher response. This creates a digital filing cabinet for students to archive their work and, in effect, creates a space for an online portfolio of work. This has a number of obvious advantages.

First, students never misplace their work. The dog never eats it; it's either in their blog or not. From a simple keeping track of papers perspective, this can make life much easier for teachers. If questions arise about whether or not a student handed in homework, the teacher can just look in the student's Weblog. (Some blogs even have time stamps on posts, so teachers can really enforce strict deadlines.)

Second, having all of their work organized in one place makes for some great opportunities for student reflection. It's very easy for students to look back over their work and, hopefully, see the growth they've accomplished. This is also true if peers, teachers, or mentors give feedback and respond in the blog. And remember that Weblogs are searchable; if a student is looking for a particular assignment or post, it's usually not too hard to locate.

Finally, work on a Weblog can be shared with others who might be interested or invested in the student's progress. Just like with a classroom portal site, it's easy for parents to follow along as a student posts his or her work. This holds true for counselors, mentors, and peers as well. It's that transparency thing again.

Now think for a moment if students had Weblogs set up from the time they started school to the time they graduated. What they could have at the end would be a comprehensive history of their work and learning that was searchable and shareable, one that would provide a great resource for reflection or future study. And it would be an artifact that students could use to show expertise in a particular vocation or to impress potential college admissions officers. Either way, having that record of learning would be a very useful thing.

E-Portfolio

It's not a huge leap to jump from blog filing cabinet to blog portfolio. The traditional portfolio process is supported almost perfectly by Weblogs. First, students collect the work they might want to consider highlighting in their portfolio and then they select those that represent their best work. (This can include links to videos, podcasts, presentations, and more, all of which we'll cover in later chapters.) They then reflect on the choices they made—something they can easily do in a blog post. Finally, they publish the result for others to see. Even more powerful is the idea that these portfolios could conceivably span many grades and many classes.

In fact, e-portfolio guru Helen Barrett created online portfolios using more than 15 different software packages, many of them Weblogs (Barrett, 2004).

Collaborative Space

One of the biggest potentials of Weblogs is the ability to create spaces where students can collaborate with others online. Although collaborative learning has been a buzzword in American education for some time now, the Read/Write Web opens up all sorts of new possibilities for students to learn from each other or from authors or scientists and other professionals who can now work side by side in digital space even though they may be far away from one another physically.

It was collaboration between my junior and senior students and Sue Monk Kidd, the author of the best-selling *The Secret Life of Bees* (Kidd, 2002) that really sold me on the potential and power of Weblogs as a learning tool (see Figure 2.3). Our school adopted the book into the curriculum just nine months after it had been released, and because it was so new, I thought to use a Weblog to have my students create an online reader's guide to the book. In the process, I contacted the book's publicist to see if the author might want to join us in our study of the book. Much to my delight, after a few back-and-forth e-mails explaining what a Weblog was and how it worked, she agreed. So, while my students read and commented online, Sue Monk Kidd was able to follow along and then respond to a series of questions they had at the end of the book. Her 2,300-word response really floored us all. It started this way:

Dear Students,

It is an exceptionally nice honor to have you reading my novel in your Modern American Literature class! I'm extremely impressed with your Weblog, which I've been following. What fun for the author to listen in on your discussions and see the wonderful and provocative artistic interpretations that you've created. The experience has opened my eyes to new ideas about my own work! (Gitty, 2002)

She went on to describe how the characters were formed, where the symbols came from, and how she came to write many of the important scenes in the book. These were insights that no one but my students (and anyone else who had stumbled onto the blog) were able to benefit from.

Since then, students at my old school have collaborated with Pulitzer Prize–winning journalists, elementary school kids in Georgia, high school students in Poland, theater troupes in Oklahoma, and the list goes on. They've shared text, pictures, audio, and video, and they've engaged in some real learning from each other. In short, the blog has allowed students to build a community around their collaborations, and it has enhanced the depth of the curriculum.

Figure 2.3   A Weblog as a Learning Tool in American Literature

Knowledge Management and Articulation

Not every use of Weblogs in schools has to involve students. In fact, blogs are a great way of communicating internally as well. School committees and groups that meet on a regular basis can use a blog to archive minutes of meetings, continue dialogues between get-togethers, share links to relevant information, and store documents and presentations for easy access later on. They are a great way to manage and communicate the knowledge that gets created.

In addition, districts can use Weblogs as articulation tools to highlight and share best practices, lesson plans, and "learning objects" such as worksheets or projects. Teachers no longer have to be in the same room to discuss what is and isn't working in their classrooms.

School Web Site

Finally, Weblogs can be used as a building block for a school Web site. A major complaint about school Web sites is that few of them are updated on a regular basis. That's an easy fix with a Weblog site. Imagine if each department had its own blog that it could maintain as needed. Imagine if all the clubs and activities, all the sports teams, and all the student government bodies had their own sites that they could update. The overall school site would move from a static, wait-for-the-Webmaster-to-update-it type site to a dynamic, every-day-there's-something-new type site.

Take a look at the Meriwether-Lewis Elementary School site, for instance (lcwiselementary.org; see Figure 2.4). Principal Tim Lauer, who is an ed-blogging pioneer in his own right, has used Weblogs to increase communication with parents and staff, post pictures and student work, keep the yearly calendar, and really create a community around the site. Teachers post weekly "Classroom Notes" that serve as a running diary of what students are doing and achieving.

Now that's not to say that everyone should be given carte blanche to post whatever they think is interesting. It's a good idea to designate a site "master" for each blog who reviews content before it gets published. And it's also a good idea to have at least one person who sees everything that goes up. (This is easier than it sounds with RSS, as I'll discuss in Chapter 5.) But there is no doubt that students, teachers, parents, and community members will all be better served by having up-to-date, relevant information at their fingertips through a Weblog or Web site.

This is by no means the definitive list of how to use blogs. In fact, educators are using them in many creative ways, from creating a portal to the school library to using them as a collaborative reflection space for new teachers and their mentors, to professional development sites for staff. As Anne Davis likes to say, "The possibilities are endless!"

Figure 2.4 Principal Tim Lauer uses a Weblog as his school Web site.

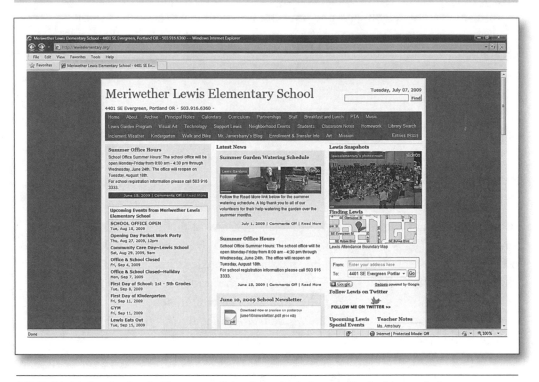

SOURCE: Meriwether Lewis Elementary School, Portland, Oregon. Used with permission.

THE PEDAGOGY OF WEBLOGS

So what exactly can Weblogs do to improve student learning? Why should classroom teachers consider blogs as a tool to deliver their curriculum? The Read/Write Web is still in its relative infancy, and the answers to these questions are just now beginning to be clarified. But there are some basic aspects of blogs that make them an attractive addition to the teacher's toolbox nonetheless.

First, Weblogs are truly a constructivist tool for learning. Because the content that students and teachers create is on the World Wide Web, it is content that becomes a part of the wider body of knowledge that the Internet represents. It is searchable; people can find it and use it. *The Secret Life of Bees* Weblog that my students created has been accessed more than 3 million times as of this writing. Needless to say, not all of those people came from our school.

That potential audience is one of the most important aspects of the Read/Write Web. The idea that the relevance of student work no longer ends at the classroom door can not only be a powerful motivator but can also create a significant shift in the way we think about the assignments and work we ask of our students in the first place.

Second, Weblogs truly expand the walls of the classroom. The Internet has always provided the possibility of connecting students with others outside the classroom via e-mail and chat groups. But now that collaboration can be much more accessible and much more diverse. We can create sites where classes from disparate geographies can conduct all sorts of experiments; share the results through text, picture, audio, or video; and invite expert scientists into the process to reflect on the results. And in a world that is moving more and more toward a business model of the collaborative construction of content, learning to work with far-flung collaborators is becoming an important literacy.

Third, blogs archive the learning that teachers and students do, facilitating all sorts of reflection and metacognitive analysis that was previously much more cumbersome. From an organizational standpoint, the ability to keep histories of work in an organized, searchable, easily shareable space is an important development.

Fourth, the Weblog is a democratic tool that supports different learning styles. For those students who might be more reticent in class, a blog gives them the opportunity to share in writing the ideas they may be too shy to speak. Everyone has a voice in the conversation, and all ideas, even the instructor's, are given equal presentation in the blog. As students participate, they also take ownership of the space, and depending on how teachers frame that participation, this can lead to a greater sense of participation.

Fifth, the use of Weblogs can enhance the development of expertise in a particular subject. Students who blog in educational settings usually focus their reading and writing on one topic, which helps bring about topic-specific expertise. A student who uses a blog to track stories and reflections on the genocide in Darfur, for example, is creating a database of learning that she can continue to build on.

Finally, blogs can teach students the new literacies they will need to function in an ever-expanding information society. The extent of our collective knowledge doubles every 18 months (Olofson, 1999), and as more and more information comes online, it's imperative that we give our students the skills to analyze and manage it. The act of writing in a Weblog, or "blogging," can go a long way toward teaching skills such as research, organization, and the synthesis of ideas.

In fact, research on the effects of Weblogs on K–12 students is still in its infancy. But the anecdotal results reported by many of the educator bloggers discussed here give broad outlines to a picture that will no doubt soon come into focus. In general, students at all levels show more interest in their work, and their ability to locate and reflect upon their work is greatly enhanced, as are the opportunities for collaborative learning.

A New Writing Genre

Posting to a Weblog can take many forms. Students can write about personal reactions to topics covered in class, post links, write reflectively, and summarize or annotate readings. They can use blogs as journals or as places to publish creative writing for larger audiences. The possibilities really are endless. But by their very structure, blogs facilitate what I think is a new genre that could be called "connective writing," a form that forces those who do it to read carefully and critically, that demands clarity and cogency in its construction, that is done for a wide audience, and that links to the sources of the ideas expressed. In essence, we write not just to communicate but to connect with others who can potentially teach us more.

Before getting further into this discussion, let's take a look at a sample blog post by then 14-year-old Arthur in Vermont. Arthur has become an accomplished blogger in his own right by writing frequently about the technologies that interest him and the implications for his own learning. Here's an example:

> In a dramatic move, the pioneer of the (new) way we get reading material has stepped up the game in how we read. Amazon has announced a revolutionary e-book reader, called Kindle. Though many have tried to revolutionize reading before, I think Amazon has a far greater chance of doing so. After all, Amazon does run the best bookstore in the world. There's all the great features you would expect from an electronic book, including mobile purchasing, search, and annotating. Most important of all, Kindle is just plain readable. By using E Ink, which actually manipulates chemicals to reduce eyestrain, one can sit down and read through the entirety of War and Peace without having to get glasses. (Especially since text size is resizable for you aging baby boomers and you can get about 30 hours of battery life to a charge.)
>
> Newsweek does a very good job of summarizing what is amazing & scary about Kindle. I think the most important thing to see is that the loop is finally completed—every step of the writing/publishing/reading process can now be done digitally (easily).
>
> Computers may have taken over every other stage of the process—the tools of research, composition and production—but that final mile of the process, where the reader mind melds with the

author in an exquisite asynchronous tango, would always be sacro-sanct, said the holdouts.

However, the article does lead into some ideas that I don't nec-essarily agree with—that writing will become a collaborative, wiki-ized effort.

"The possibility of interaction will redefine authorship," says Peter Brantley, executive director of the Digital Library Federation, an association of libraries and institutions. Unlike some writing-in-public advocates, he doesn't spare the novelists. "Michael Chabon will have to rethink how he writes for this medium," he says. Brantley envisions wiki-style collaborations where the author, instead of being the sole authority, is a "super user," the lead wolf of a creative pack.

The reason that I buy books is that they are blatantly one person's thoughts upon a subject or one person's story—one lone person's perspective. I enjoy curling up with a book and reading what a lone crusader has written. However, I do see lots of potential in the annotation of our reading—contrasting/additional thoughts clearly marked as contrasting/additional thoughts.

Jim Gerber, Google's content-partnerships director, suggests that it might be an interesting idea, for example, for someone on the lib-eral side of the fence to annotate an Ann Coulter book, providing refuting links for every contention that the critic thought was an inaccurate representation. That commentary, perhaps bolstered and updated by anyone who wants to chime in, could be woven into the book itself, if you chose to include it.

Despite all this, I don't believe that Kindle will be the device to truly revolutionize reading. Instead, I think a more all-around device will prove to be the future of reading. Perhaps the XO? (Especially/already in Africa) What do you think? Will the Kindle become the "iPod of reading?" (Pell, 2007)

As that example shows, connective writing is, for the most part, exposi-tory writing, but the process starts with reading. In fact, that is the biggest shift, I think, in the way we need to approach reading and writing for our students and ourselves. As University of Connecticut professor Donald Leu says, "Online reading and writing are so closely connected that it is not pos-sible to separate them; we read online as authors and we write online as read-ers" (Leu, O'Byrne, Zawilinski, McVerry, & Everett-Cocapardo, 2007, p. 266). And Deborah Brandt, from the University of Wisconsin-Madison, echoes this when she says students "[are] going to be reading, but they're going to be reading to write, and not to be shaped by what they read" (as cited in Keller, 2009).

Remember the origin of the Weblog? It was a list of the sites that someone had visited and, presumably, read. But more than just reading, bloggers that write in this way learn to read critically, because as they read, they look for important ideas to write about. It's an important first step, for as Samuel Johnson said, "I hate to read a writer who has written more than he has read."

This, in turn, requires critical thinking skills as writers consider their audience and clarify the purpose of the writing. Many times, one post is the synthesis of the reading of many texts, so bloggers must be able to find connections and articulate the relevance of those connections. In composing the post, this genre of writing demands organization and clarity as well as a keen awareness of audience. Also expected is the writer's own reflections on, or experience with, the ideas she's writing about.

Throughout this process, bloggers are constantly making editorial decisions, and these decisions are more complex than those made when writing for a limited audience. Because students are regularly selecting content to include or link to, they must learn to find and identify accurate and trustworthy sources of information. Because of a potential audience that goes beyond the classroom, they pay more attention to the editorial correctness of the post as well.

Although it may seem that the final step in the process is to finally publish the post to the Weblog, this connective writing genre actually continues past publication. That's because of the ability of readers to interact with the post, another example of the connective aspect of it. This is a crucial distinction that necessarily changes the purpose of the writing. When I post to my Weblog, I anticipate the reader's response as much as I can, but ultimately, my post is still a draft, a way to test my best ideas and writing against an audience. When readers do respond or give feedback, blogging continues. Take Morgante's post above as an example. In the 14 comments from readers that followed, the conversation deepens, widens, and our potential learning increases. In fact, some would argue that a true blog post is never really finished, that as long as it's out there for others to interact with, the potential for deeper insight exists. Konrad Glogowski, a fourth-grade teacher from Ontario, says that his students see this type of blogging "as transactional writing, as writing to be interacted with, to be returned to and reflected upon" (Glogowski, 2005). In fact, comments are a powerful motivator of student writing in blogs, especially when those comments come from sources outside of the classroom walls. So, we have to stop thinking of publication as the end of the process; if anything, in the social writing space of blogs, it's a midpoint.

The differences between blogging in this manner and writing as we traditionally think of it are clear: Writing stops; blogging continues. Writing is inside; blogging is outside. Writing is monologue; blogging is conversation.

Writing is thesis; blogging is synthesis . . . none of which minimizes the importance of writing. But writing becomes an ongoing process, one that is not just done for the contrived purposes of the classroom. Ken Smith, a writing instructor at Indiana University, puts it this way:

> Instead of assigning students to go write, we should assign them to go read and then link to what interests them and write about why it does and what it means, not in order to make a connection or build social capital but because it is through quality linking . . . that one first comes in contact with the essential acts of blogging: close reading and interpretation. Blogging, at base, is writing down what you think when you read others. If you keep at it, others will eventually write down what they think when they read you, and you'll enter a new realm of blogging, a new realm of human connection. (Smith, 2004)

That's a pretty powerful vision of what blogging can be.

Doing connective writing in blogs, then, is a different experience than just posting. If we take a look at the spectrum of different types of Weblog posts, we can start to see where posting ends and blogging as an academic exercise begins:

1. Posting assignments. (Not blogging.)

2. Journaling, i.e., "This is what I did today." (Not blogging.)

3. Posting links. (Not blogging.)

4. Links with descriptive annotation, i.e., "This site is about. . . ." (Not really blogging either, but getting close depending on the depth of the description.)

5. Links with analysis that gets into the meaning of the content being linked. (A simple form of blogging.)

6. Reflective, metacognitive writing on practice without links. (Complex writing, but simple blogging, I think. Commenting would probably fall in here somewhere.)

7. Links with analysis and synthesis that articulate a deeper understanding or relationship to the content being linked and written with potential audience response in mind. (Real blogging.)

8. Extended analysis and synthesis over a longer period of time that builds on previous posts, links, and comments. (Complex blogging.)

A quick look at the "Standards for the Language Arts" written by the National Council of Teachers of English (NCTE) also suggests the potential of Weblogs as a classroom tool (see the end of this chapter). In almost every one of the twelve standards, blogs have obvious relevance, whether it's that "Students employ a wide range of strategies as they write and use different writing process elements appropriately to communicate with different audiences for a variety of purposes," something bloggers do by the very nature of their process, or "Students participate as knowledgeable, reflective, creative, and critical members of a variety of literacy communities" (NCTE, 2009). Blogs create and connect these communities like few other tools.

And from a reading and writing literacy standpoint, NCTE's "Definition of Twenty-First Century Literacies" should also add some fuel to the using-blogs-in-the-classrooms fire (NCTE, 2008). Among other things, readers and writers in the twenty-first century should be able to "build relationships with others to pose and solve problems collaboratively and cross-culturally," and "design and share information for global communities to meet a variety of purposes" (NCTE, 2008). If we are looking at blogs as one way to help our students begin to build connections (and not simply publish), they'll be well on their way to becoming literate for their era.

Scaffolding Blogging

How then to introduce this new genre to students? When is an appropriate age to begin teaching our students the skills that blogging encompasses? Certainly, elementary students could not be expected to do the consistent analytical thinking and writing that extended blogging requires. But to start, we could provide or ask students to find interesting and relevant sites of information and teach them how to write about what they find useful at those sites. We could ask them to do some basic deconstruction of the design of the site, or we could ask them to write about what more they would like to see. Even at this level, teachers may consider recruiting an audience to interact with students, allowing them to begin exploring what it means to write with an ear for readership and to enter into conversations about ideas. And it's never too early to start thinking about bringing primary sources like authors, scientists, politicians, and the like into the classroom through the blog so students can ask questions and reflect on the answers. But there's also nothing wrong with asking other teachers, friends, or even parents to become a part of the learning as well.

Middle school students might be asked to work at becoming "experts" about topics that they care about by using blogs. They might be ready to compare information from different sources and to reflect on their process of determining which sources are trustworthy and which are not. Again, structuring ways to include reader response is an important ingredient in helping to develop blogging skills.

Older students can be asked to begin using Weblogs for extended study and reflection on a topic. They could be asked to reflect and build on previous ideas, incorporate feedback from readers, synthesize readings from a number of different sources, and advance new ideas or interpretations of the topic.

This is just one way to think about the introduction of blogging as a viable and valuable writing genre in the classroom. The thousands of educators who are now entering the blogosphere will certainly provide us with many more creative examples in years to come.

BLOGGING ACROSS THE CURRICULUM

Although the nature of Weblogs makes them fairly obvious tools for teaching writing and reading, educators are using blogs in all areas of the curriculum to collaborate with subject-specific experts, to archive learning, to share results of experiments, and to publish student work. Blogging across the curriculum offers students and teachers not only the ability to infuse writing into all disciplines, it facilitates connections in ways that plain paper cannot. Students can work on math problems with peers from other classes. Science experiments can be run concurrently at any number of different sites across the country or around the world with student researchers comparing and reflecting on the results on a Weblog. Language students can create conversations with native speakers, physical education students can log and analyze their workouts or diets, and history students can construct resource sites for their study of ancient civilizations and conflicts.

Here are a few specific examples of teachers employing Weblogs with their students.

AP Calculus (tinyurl.com/2v4862)

Darren Kuropatwa (2005) is a math teacher from Winnipeg who uses a Weblog as a starting point for the introduction of new concepts, a place to share links and ideas with his students, and a forum for discussion about the class (see Figure 2.5). The subtitle of the site says it all: "A window through the walls of our classroom. This is an interactive learning ecology for students and parents in my AP Calculus class. This ongoing dialogue is as rich as YOU make it. Visit often and post your comments freely." Darren uses Blogger software and allows his students to post to the class blog by making them all team members. (More on that in the next chapter.) He keeps his own blog at tinyurl.com/2rk83y, where he reflects on his teaching and his use of blogs. In his first post there, he writes:

> The breakneck evolution of technologies on the Internet is changing the way we teach. It's hard to keep up. I hope to use this blog to record and reflect on my personal evolution of how to integrate these technologies into my teaching. (Kuropatwa, 2005)

Figure 2.5   Darren Kuropatwa's site is a good example of how disciplines like math and science can use blogs.

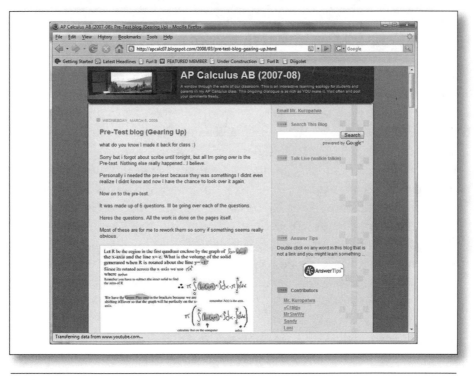

SOURCE: Used with permission of Darren Kuropatwa.

Darren's AP Calculus site has the feel of an online neighborhood where he and his students post pictures of pi-shaped structures, reflect on how to study for tests, and share what they're learning. They also include multimedia captures of their classes, social bookmarking lists, presentations, and more. One pretty typical post by a student highlights an "a-ha" moment she experienced: "Let me just say that Mr. K. doesn't put these links to be stared at. It was written to serve its purpose of helping us to learn and improve our studies. Personally I found out that it's easier for me to learn from the online quizzes than from the assignments" (as cited in Kuropatwa, 2005).

Since he began his blog program over five years ago, Darren has expanded his student connections. They have begun to mentor other calculus students in Canada and California, and they have been getting some "blog mentoring" from preservice teachers at the University of Regina. Interestingly, according to Darren, his own students have been able to teach the university students a thing or two as well. It's all about the connections.

Mr. C.'s Class Blog (tinyurl.com/clby52)

Bill Chamberlain in Noel, Missouri, has a great blog for his fifth-grade class where he not only gives his students the chance to connect to the world but he invites the world into his classroom on a regular basis. One look at his site and you can tell that this is a creative, connected teacher who uses a blog in some powerful ways. And like Darren, Bill has his own blog space where he reflects on his own use of social Web tools in his classroom and his learning (tinyurl.com/c18fys).

What's very cool is that anytime class is in session, we can watch a live stream of his classroom using Ustream (which we'll talk about later on). Why? As he writes on his blog, "I wanted to share my classroom with people outside of my school. I wanted my students to show what they were doing to anyone that wanted to see, [and] I wanted a connection to form between my students and the world" (tinyurl.com/cxvvts). One quick look at the posts in the center column and you'll see a variety of topics, multimedia, engaging comments, and a sense of the world that goes far beyond the school. His students follow other classroom blogs, which are linked on the right, and they comment and interact in those spaces on a regular basis. (In fact, every Friday is "Comment Day," since he believes comments really motivate young writers.) Finally, you get links to over a dozen different ways to connect with "Mr. C." online.

The surprising thing is that Bill has grown this site into a global portal in just a few months, and he shares a lot of his thinking (and the thinking of one of his coteachers) in a 20-minute video that I would highly recommend, especially for newcomers to these tools. (It's at tinyurl.com/qg3beq.) There he says "Collaboration between classrooms is unusual, but collaboration between classrooms in different parts of the world, literally on the other side of the world, is not something easy or possible without the technology we use."

The Write Weblog (tinyurl.com/51yr59)

As previously noted, Anne Davis is one of the true pioneers of blogs in classrooms. Her Weblog "EduBlog Insights" (tinyurl.com/61cfmo) is a great starting point for teachers wanting to see firsthand what happens when you mix blogs and students. The Write Weblog (tinyurl.com/51yr59) is a place where fifth graders chronicled their learning about writing and, from the looks of it, a lot of learning took place (see Figure 2.6). All students had their own blog where they reflected on their process and had conversations with readers, and their sites were open for anyone to read and comment on.

Like the others, Anne reflects often on her own learning through the use of Weblogs. A great example is a post called "Who Says Elementary Students Can't Blog?" in which, after discussing her process for the day in some depth, she writes, "This process of browsing, reading, learning, thinking, and selecting topics will be the first order of the day for each session. I think this is going to work out well" (Davis, 2005).

The effect on the students in the class was profound. One girl, Paulina, wrote:

One of the greatest things that happened to me was when I got chosen to have a blog. At first I thought it was just extra work, but then I started liking it. This has been a great year. We have learned

Figure 2.6   Anne Davis's "The Write Weblog" is a great example of how elementary school students can flourish using blogs.

SOURCE: Used with permission of Anne Davis.

so much and I hope that future generations will have a chance to experience what we have. (*Paulina's Club*, 2005)

Depending on the focus, Weblogs in the classroom have the potential to affect student learning in many positive ways. Blogging can teach critical reading and writing skills, and it can lead to greater information management skills. It can help students become much more media and information literate by clarifying the choices they make about the content they write about, it can teach them about how networks function—both human and computer—and it can teach the essential skill of collaboration.

BLOGS AS RESOURCES

Regardless of whether you and/or your students become bloggers, blogs have probably already become sources of information about whatever topics you might be studying. And this means that at the very least, you and your students will need to learn how to evaluate them for accuracy and trustworthiness. If anyone with an Internet connection can now get online and start blogging about any topic he or she wants, how do we know whom to believe? The easy way is to not believe any of the bloggers since their posts are, at least in the traditional ways, unedited content. But that would be to ignore some very smart and relevant voices that are gaining more and more of a reputation as credible sources each day. And really, this is the work that is required of all of us if we are to be truly information literate in the twenty-first century.

Before getting to some specific strategies for determining valid sources, I would urge you to read long-time edublogger Stephen Downes's excellent post on the topic. Essentially, Downes says that there is no way to tell for sure if something you read on the Web in general is true, and that we can no longer trust even traditional sources to always be accurate and tell the truth. In the end, "determining what to believe—or to not believe—is a matter of trust. You need to determine for yourself who to trust about what" (Downes, 2005).

I agree, and teachers and students have to realize that we've entered an age in which there are no longer many free passes when it comes to assessing the reliability of a source. As we've seen in the past few years, even the *New York Times* can get it horribly wrong, and now that everyone can have a voice in the more controversial subjects of the day, it's getting harder and harder to make sense of it all.

So, getting a handle on the reliability of Web content in general and blog content specifically takes time, much more than you or your students are used to. A first step is to try to find out as much as you can about the author of the Weblog. See if there is an "About" link that will lead to a name and some background on the author. What is her profession? What is her title? Where does her authority on the topic come from? You may want to do a name search on Google to see what comes up. Remember, though, that some bloggers prefer to stay anonymous, and although that obviously makes it difficult to use that person's ideas in research, it doesn't totally preclude it. Also, you might want to find out who owns a site by going to Internic.com and doing a search for who registered the domain name.

Next, you may want to find out what kind of a reputation the blogger has among his peers. One way to do this is to go to the blog tracking site Technorati.com and enter the URL of the blog into the search form. The results will feature an "Authority" rating that is based on how many other bloggers have linked to that particular Weblog. In general, I would say that any site that has a rating higher than 100 has earned a reputation as a good source of information by its community. But that doesn't mean that blogs with a lower rating should be discounted, just as blogs with more than 100 should not be automatically accepted. Technorati is just a first step. Students should be taught to take the time to evaluate the sites that are linking to a blog as well.

Also, take a look at the "blogroll" or list of blogs that the blogger links to. Again, try to find out as much as you can about the blogger's personal agenda, if there is one. Finally, take the time to read through some of the other posts on the site and click through to the links they include. Does the author's synthesis of what she is reading seem credible? Is there an obvious political bias or is something being sold? Are other people commenting and, if so, what are they saying?

You'll need to have these discussions with your students, many of whom will tend to use the first source they find that supports their thesis. And you'll have to develop your own standards for blog sources. Ideally, for a blog to be used as a part of a research effort, you should be able to identify who the author is, what she does for a living, what her level of expertise is, and what judgments others have made about her. Anything less renders the source unacceptable.

So, it's obvious that Weblogs are already making an impact on our curricula whether we are employing them as research tools or as publishing tools. These next few years promise to be very messy in terms of sorting through the issues of trust and reliability, but I can promise you this: becoming a blogger and blogging consistently is the absolute best way to navigate through the murkiness. There is no better way to understand the impact of the Read/Write Web than by becoming a part of it. And by the end of the next chapter, you'll be able to do just that.

CLASSROOM USES OF WEBLOGS

You might like to create a reflective, journal-type blog to

- reflect on your teaching experiences etc.,
- keep a log of teacher-training experiences etc.,
- write a description of a specific teaching unit,
- describe what worked for you in the classroom or what didn't work,
- provide some teaching tips for other teachers,
- write about something you learned from another teacher,
- explain teaching insights you gain from what happens in your classes,
- share ideas for teaching activities or language games to use in the classroom,
- provide some how-tos on using specific technology in the class, describing how you used this technology in your own class,
- explore important teaching and learning issues.

You might like to start a class blog to

- post class-related information such as calendars, events, homework assignments, and other pertinent class information;
- post assignments based on literature readings and have students respond on their own Weblogs, creating a kind of portfolio of their work;
- communicate with parents if you are teaching elementary school students;
- post prompts for writing;
- provide examples of classwork, vocabulary activities, or grammar games;
- provide online readings for your students to read and react to;
- gather and organize Internet resources for a specific course, providing links to appropriate sites and annotating the links as to what is relevant about them;
- post photos and comment on class activities;
- invite student comments or postings on issues in order to give them a writing voice;
- publish examples of good student writing done in class;
- showcase student art, poetry, and creative stories;
- create a dynamic teaching site, posting not only class-related information, but also activities, discussion topics, links to additional information about topics they are studying in class, and readings to inspire learning;

- create a literature circle (where groups of students read and discuss the same book);
- create an online book club;
- make use of the commenting feature to have students publish messages on topics being used to develop language skills;
- ask students to create their own individual course blogs, where they can post their own ideas, reactions, and written work;
- post tasks to carry out project-based learning tasks with students;
- build a class newsletter, using student-written articles and photos they take;
- link your class with another class somewhere else in the world.

You can encourage your students (either on your Weblog using the comments feature or on their own Weblogs) to blog

- their reactions to thought-provoking questions,
- their reactions to photos you post,
- journal entries,
- results of surveys they carry out as part of a class unit,
- their ideas and opinions about topics discussed in class.

You can have your students create their own Weblogs to

- learn how to blog;
- complete class writing assignments;
- create an ongoing portfolio of samples of their writing;
- express their opinions on topics you are studying in class;
- write comments, opinions, or questions on daily news items or issues of interest;
- discuss activities they did in class and tell what they think about them (you, the teacher, can learn a lot this way);
- write about class topics, using newly learned vocabulary words and idioms;
- showcase their best writing pieces.

You can also ask your class to create a shared Weblog to

- complete project work in small groups, assigning each group a different task;
- showcase products of project-based learning;
- complete a WebQuest (an online, structured research activity);
- share ideas you have for using Weblogs in education (tinyurl .com/6jvojy).

STANDARDS FOR THE ENGLISH LANGUAGE ARTS SPONSORED BY NCTE AND IRA

The vision guiding these standards is that all students must have the opportunities and resources to develop the language skills they need to pursue life's goals and to participate fully as informed, productive members of society. These standards assume that literacy growth begins before children enter school as they experience and experiment with literacy activities—reading and writing, and associating spoken words with their graphic representations. Recognizing this fact, these standards encourage the development of curriculum and instruction that make productive use of the emerging literacy abilities that children bring to school. Furthermore, the standards provide ample room for the innovation and creativity essential to teaching and learning. They are not prescriptions for particular curriculum or instruction. Although we present these standards as a list, we want to emphasize that they are not distinct and separable; they are, in fact, interrelated and should be considered as a whole.

1. Students read a wide range of print and nonprint texts to build an understanding of texts, of themselves, and of the cultures of the United States and the world; to acquire new information; to respond to the needs and demands of society and the workplace; and for personal fulfillment. Among these texts are fiction and nonfiction, and classic and contemporary works.

2. Students read a wide range of literature from many periods in many genres to build an understanding of the many dimensions (philosophical, ethical, aesthetic) of human experience.

3. Students apply a wide range of strategies to comprehend, interpret, evaluate, and appreciate texts. They draw on their prior experience, their interactions with other readers and writers, their knowledge of word meaning and of other texts, their word identification strategies, and their understanding of textual features (such as sound-letter correspondence, sentence structure, context, graphics).

4. Students adjust their use of spoken, written, and visual language (conventions, style, vocabulary) to communicate effectively with a variety of audiences and for different purposes.

5. Students employ a wide range of strategies as they write and use different writing process elements appropriately to communicate with different audiences for a variety of purposes.

6. Students apply knowledge of language structure, language conventions (like spelling and punctuation), media techniques, figurative language, and genre to create, critique, and discuss print and nonprint texts.

7. Students conduct research on issues and interests by generating ideas and questions, and by posing problems. They gather, evaluate, and synthesize data from a variety of sources (print and nonprint texts, artifacts, people) to communicate their discoveries in ways that suit their purpose and audience.

8. Students use a variety of technological and information resources (libraries, databases, computer networks, video) to gather and synthesize information and to create and communicate knowledge.

9. Students develop an understanding of and respect for diversity in language use, patterns, and dialects across cultures, ethnic groups, geographic regions, and social roles.

10. Students whose first language is not English make use of their first language to develop competency in the English language arts and to develop understanding of content across the curriculum.

11. Students participate as knowledgeable, reflective, creative, and critical members of a variety of literacy communities.

12. Students use spoken, written, and visual language to accomplish their own purposes (for example, for learning, enjoyment, persuasion, and the exchange of information).

SOURCE: *Standards for the English Language Arts,* by the International Reading Association and the National Council of Teachers of English. Copyright 1996 by the International Reading Association and the National Council of Teachers of English. Reprinted with permission.

3 Weblogs

Get Started!

S o if you believe, as I do, that Weblogs can play an important role in your classroom, then it's time to start thinking about the ways you can most effectively implement them for your own unique purposes.

The true potential of blogs in schools comes when students and teachers use them as publishing tools. And, to me at least, the best way to fully understand the potential of Weblogs as a teaching and learning tool is to become a blogger. Just as writing teachers should write, and literature teachers should read, teachers who use blogs should, well, use blogs. Without question, the most profound learning experience of my life has been the ongoing education I have received by keeping my own Weblog for the past seven years. The process of blogging and my use of the other tools that the Read/Write Web has spawned have not only made writing a daily part of my life, they have changed the way that I read and consume information.

Former Middlebury College professor Barbara Ganley, who used Weblogs extensively in her courses, wrote, "How can a teacher expect her students to blog (or to use any other tool, strategy, or technique) if she doesn't use it herself, exploring the impact it has on her thinking, writing, research, and creativity?" (Ganley, 2004b). She also says:

> And as we all know, when a teacher believes in what she's doing and is confident in her tools, well, it rubs off on even the most resistant of students. As reflective research-teachers, we must continue to circle back and look at how what we do ties into our long-term educational goals. (Ganley, 2004a)

I agree. If we want our students to learn from blogs, we have to experience that learning firsthand or, as Ganley says, "get into their shoes."

Even more, I think teachers should blog to show students that it is something of value and to model appropriate ways of doing it. Remember, millions of kids are already blogging, so they certainly are enticed by the tool. But very few are using their sites as places of critical thinking, analytical writing and reflection, and all the rest of those NCTE literacies discussed in Chapter 2. It's well and good to encourage and teach our students to blog, but they will surely give it up at the end of the semester unless we've shown them why it's important to keep writing and to keep learning. (No pressure.)

Getting started with blogging from a technical aspect is not difficult, and in a bit we'll talk about the easiest ways to begin. But from the perspective of writing for an audience and getting into the habit of regular reflection, it does take some effort to get the blog rolling, so to speak. The first step is to take some time to just read some good Weblogs. A good place to find some that might interest you is at SupportBlogging.com, or you can look at the short list at the end of this chapter. (And don't forget the Edublogs Award site at tinyurl.com/62crba.) Remember as well that reading Weblogs is a different type of reading than what you've previously done. Unlike books or newspaper and magazine articles, most blog posts are fairly short. There are links inviting you to investigate other sources. And most importantly, you can engage in a dialogue about the topic by reading the comments and, perhaps, leaving your own. In fact, posting on other people's blogs before you start your own is a great way to get the feel of publishing your thoughts. Just wait until that first person responds to something you've written; that's when you'll truly start to understand the power of the Read/Write Web.

START SMALL

When you're ready to begin your own blog, you might want to start small by using the first few posts to just create a link to something interesting that you've read along with a short excerpt, nothing more. You won't truly be "blogging," as described in the previous chapter, but you'll be getting a feel for the experience of publishing online, and you'll be scaffolding your blogging in similar ways to your students. When you get comfortable with the process, you may want to begin annotating the links you post with a couple of sentences that highlight what you think is meaningful or important about what you've read. As you get more settled into the rhythm of posting, begin to write more in depth about what you are reading, drawing on your own personal experiences and reflections. In this way, you'll come to understand the true mental work that is blogging. These types of posts should form the foundation of your blog work. That's not to say keeping a blog is all work and no play, however. Don't be afraid to include some posts that are totally personal or just for fun; your readers want to see the person behind the blog as well.

Another piece of advice: Be a public blogger. Put your name on your work, but make sure you understand the ramifications of doing so. Different schools have different comfort levels with teachers' blogging, and I try to think very carefully about what I write about my own school in my blog. Remember, this is a learning tool and may not necessarily be the place where you want to air your complaints about the board of education, parents, or particular students. Public writing demands discretion, especially in an educational setting. And remember too that what you write stays with you. Each post contributes to your online portfolio, which may turn up in future Google searches.

BLOGGING WITH STUDENTS

So, once you've become a blogger and you've decided to try Weblogs in your teaching practice, what's the best way to start? Obviously, before planning your blog work, you need to consider the level of Internet access that your students have both at school and at home. According to the U.S. Census, household Internet connections jumped to 62 percent, up from 17 percent just 10 years ago. And, estimates are that about 70 percent of homes will have broadband access by 2012 (Jupiter Research, 2007). The bad news is that until those numbers reach 100 percent, Weblogs will be out of reach for some teachers and students in this country. Although you can use blogs even if students don't have outside access to the Web, the possibilities for their use are much greater if they do.

Regardless of the level of connectivity, however, and as I advised earlier with your own use, I would start small. The most obvious initial implementation is first to use Weblogs as a place to post homework assignments and relevant class links. Don't worry about collaborations or conversations at the outset. Just get used to how it feels to communicate information to your students online, and let your students get used to consuming that information in a different form. Let parents know that you've created a site for your class materials, and give them whatever information they need to get regular updates.

First, get students reading blogs. Prepare a list of Weblogs with appropriate content and look at some of those sites with your students. You may even want to show your own site. But because good blogging starts with good reading, it's important that you provide some models for them to look at and follow. With younger students, you may want to show what other elementary schools are doing, whereas with older students you may want to pick a few bloggers whom you've read and come to respect. Again, see the accompanying list for some suggestions.

Next, you may want to try letting students respond to the posts on your class blog. The first time I used Weblogs with one of my classes, I posted a question each day that I wanted them to think about and discuss after school.

I asked them to make a certain number of responses to the questions during the week, and we modeled what the expectations were for those responses beforehand. I made sure the questions were sufficiently provocative, and most of my students went way beyond the required number of responses. It gave them a great opportunity to experience public writing in a safe way and to get the posting process down.

Having small groups of students actually start creating posts to the same Weblog is a great way to introduce them to blogging (in the "connective writing" sense) and to help them understand the process. Again, be very clear as to what your expectations are, and just as with any other writing genre, spend some time teaching them how to blog. Use your own blog as a model.

Finally, you may want to consider giving each student his or her own blog. But before you do, make sure you and your students are totally comfortable with the technology and with the concept of reading and working online. Although there's no doubt that more and more content will be created and consumed online in years to come, some have not yet done enough reading online to be totally comfortable with it. Giving each student a Weblog basically means a paperless classroom.

And giving them their own site invites a discussion of how much of that site should be their own. By that I mean can they add pictures and quotes of their liking, much as they might to their notebooks or lockers? Can they do journal-type writing that might be unrelated to the coursework? Can they write about their own passions regardless of whether or not those passions have any relevance to the curriculum? These types of questions might be negotiated with the students themselves. Although I believe that allowing students to personalize their spaces makes them more invested in their blogs, I also feel that it makes the assessment more difficult.

BLOG SAFETY

Regardless of how you start using Weblogs with students, make sure that students, parents, and even administrators are clear about the expectations and the reasoning behind it. And make sure everyone has the proper permissions. At our school, and as shared in Chapter 1, we made publishing to the Web a part of our Acceptable Use Policy that parents had to sign. I'd also encourage you to communicate to parents what safety precautions you have in place to protect student privacy. On the K–12 levels, this may mean using only first names of students, or even pseudonyms for students with unique names. It means teaching kids never to publish personal identifiers about themselves or others. It means making sure they know the process for reporting problems in their blogs, whether technical or content related. It means doing professional development for staff that clarifies the uses and purposes of blogs. The more documentation and backup you have from students, parents, and administrators in terms of clarifying the use of the tool the better. Bud Hunt, an educational technologist in Colorado and a well-read edublogger, has a great resource for documents of these types at his "Blogging Policies and Resources Wiki" (tinyurl.com/5y919n). And safety also means having in place a way to consistently monitor the activity on whatever blogs your students are using. I'll show you an easy way to do that in the chapter about RSS (Chapter 5).

When overseeing student blogs, the teacher's role becomes that of connector, not just evaluator. As you read what students write, try to respond by commenting back when appropriate. And link to the best student posts and ideas in the class blog. This is a very important habit to form. When you celebrate good work, or use students' unique ideas to drive further discussion, it goes a long way toward creating a community of learners. Anne Davis is great at doing this, as her post titled "Tips from TheWriteTeam" shows: "Your posts today were excellent! I just had to pull one from each of you to share on our class blog. Here goes!" (Davis, 2005). She goes on to expertly weave together excerpts from all of her student blogs so they can easily see the things their peers are writing about and feel that sense of accomplishment that Anne so wonderfully imbues.

Assessing Weblog use can be as easy as counting the number of blog posts a student publishes or as complicated as reading each post for form and content. I think it's unreasonable to grade every post that a student might make, but it may be reasonable to include every post in some overall assessment of effort. Also, students can self-select their best blogging posts, reflect on those selections, and include those reflections in an overall evaluation of their Weblog use. I've used a rubric to generally assess student work in the blog that evaluates the level of participation, the intellectual depth of the posts, the effectiveness of the writing, the level of reflection regarding the ideas expressed, and the willingness to contribute to and collaborate with the work of others.

What happens to the blog after the course ends is largely up to how the blogs are being hosted and what district policy is in place. If students will continue to be able to have access to the sites, you may want to send a note home informing parents that this is the case. If you plan to take the sites down at the end of the year, give students a chance to save their work or perhaps transfer it to another service if possible.

BLOG SOFTWARE

From a software standpoint, a few basic considerations apply. If you are thinking about a software program that requires installation on a local server, you will want to make sure you have adequate tech support on hand to address any problems that may arise. Depending on what you choose, you or your support people may need to learn how to maintain the installation, back up the files on the server, and stay current on the latest updates. If you don't think you have enough tech support to run the program, you'll need to consider either going with a package that offers free hosting or purchasing hosting offsite from one of any number of Weblog suppliers. (More on specific programs later in this chapter.)

Regardless of what software you use, plan to take some time to dig into it and learn what its capabilities are. Even though most Weblog software makes it easy to get up and running, there are limitations as to the levels of security, collaboration, and ability to upload files. And if you're thinking about introducing Weblogs on a wide scale, plan to run small-group training sessions of six to ten people at a time. Know, too, that documentation for most blogging packages is pretty slim. You might want to use your blog to keep track of the how-to information you dig up or come across in your travels.

The good news from a budget standpoint is that many blogging sites on the Internet offer their services for free, and there are a number of viable open-source packages that can be hosted locally. Blogging doesn't have to break the bank. Again, the trade-offs are level of security and ability to easily monitor what's being posted.

BLOGGING STEP BY STEP

So, from the technical side, what's the best way to start blogging? Unfortunately, the perfect edublogging program has yet to be written, so this answer depends on what your needs and plans are.

For a personal blog, and from an ease-of-use standpoint, I would recommend Blogger (www.Blogger.com), which is owned by Google (see Figure 3.1). Blogger will host your Weblog for free, so you don't need to worry about setting up or maintaining software. It's also one of the easiest to use, and it has some levels of privacy that may make it worthy of consideration for a class blog as well. In fact, many teachers have used Blogger with their students with great success. Remember, you can create as many blogs at Blogger as you want from your one account, so you could manage a number of different sites from the one Blogger "dashboard."

Signing up for a blog at Blogger is as easy as advertised. Remember—when you fill in your "Display Name" in the process, consider using your full, real name so that you'll become more "clickable" or findable by other learners out there. The address of your site will be "whatevernameyouchoose .blogspot.com," so give some thought to what you want the first part of that

Figure 3.1 Just click the arrow on the Blogger homepage to get started.

SOURCE: Used with permission of Google Inc.

address to be, and be ready to try a few times to get a unique address that no one else has already chosen. Once you get through the sign-up process the first time, remember that you can always create another site by using the "Create a Blog" button on the dashboard that comes up after you login.

When you click on a blog name from the dashboard, you'll be taken to the page where you can create and edit posts depending on which tab is selected (as shown in Figure 3.2).

Just hit the "New Post" button to, well, create a new post to the homepage (Figure 3.3).

You'll be shown a form that has a line for a title and then a box for the post itself. Make sure you have the "Compose" tab on the top right of the box selected as this will give you the WYSIWYG (What You See Is What You Get) editor. Just give your post a title, enter in your content, format and create links by using the fairly standard icons along the top, decide if you want people to be able to comment, and then choose to either "Save Now" as a draft for editing later or publish it directly to your blog.

Figure 3.2 Creating content on Blogger is as easy as clicking the "Create a New Post" button.

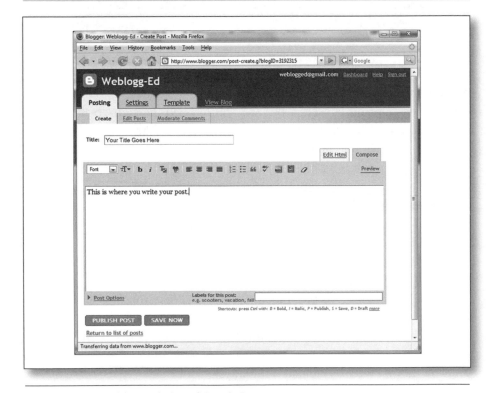

SOURCE: Used with permission of Google Inc.

Figure 3.3 If you can create an e-mail, you can create a blog post.

SOURCE: Used with permission of Google Inc.

And there is a "Blogger for Word" tool now that allows you to post right to your blog from Microsoft Word (tinyurl.com/brp74). The good news is that this gives you the ability to spell-check your post before publishing it, and it gives you an easy way of saving your work locally. Be aware, however, that not all of the formatting capabilities in Word will translate over to your Blogger site. And, for you iPhone users, you might want to download the BlogPress app for $2.99 (tinyurl.com/6ceyx6). You can upload pictures, text, create links, and more, all from your phone. (This also works with other blogging platforms.) So now, blogging is a mobile activity as well.

A note about comments: Under the "Settings" tab, there is a link to configure how you want your comments to work. There are four options: only registered users of Blogger (which Blogger hopes you'll check so they get more registered users), anyone who might read your post, anyone with a Google account, or only people who are registered members of your blog. For that last one, remember that you have complete control over who those members are, as you are the one who invites them. (This is done by clicking the "Permissions" link under the "Settings" tab and then going through the "Add Authors" process.) So if you are thinking about a blog that you can use to collaborate with colleagues, or even students, that might be the best option you choose.

With student use, although Blogger does not directly give teachers the ability to approve student posts before publication, there is a way to work around this: Have students save all posts as "drafts" until they get the teacher's go ahead to publish. Or, the teacher could press the "publish" button himself. That way, nothing goes online without consent. Remember, however, for this to work, the teacher has to have full access to all student sites (not a bad idea no matter what blog software you use). In Blogger, go to "Permissions" under the "Settings" tab and make sure the teacher/member is checked as an author as well.

You can always edit posts that you have created, even ones that you have published to the site, though most bloggers try not to do this. All of the posts on the site can be found under the "Edit Post" link under the "Posting" tab. You can even search your posts there, and you can choose to show as many posts as you want on that page.

The "Template" tab is where you would go should you want to roll up your sleeves and start changing the look of your page. Under the "Page Elements" section, you can add lists of links, polls, pictures, and even videos in the area surrounding the blog posts themselves. Just click on the "Add a Page Element" or any of the other "Edit" links in the sample template and you can do a lot to start to personalize your blog. Or, if you want to get your hands dirty with HTML, you can go in and tweak the template code itself. But if you do this, be careful! The Blogger template has all sorts of code in it that makes your site work, and if you change any of it, you may render it inoperable. I would always suggest that if you're going to start playing with the template you first copy and paste the current, working code into a document that you can use to repair whatever you might mess up.

ADDING PICTURES AND MORE TO BLOG POSTS

Adding pictures to your blog is easy since Blogger gives you over one gigabyte of space on their server per blog. Just click on the image icon on the posting form and you'll be taken to a page where you can select pictures from your hard drive to include in the post (see Figure 3.4). Remember that your photos should be sized and formatted *before* you upload them. So if you need to rotate a picture or crop it, do so before letting Blogger take a copy of it. On the same page, you can also choose the URL of a picture that's already on the Web. (You can find the URL by right clicking on any Web image and selecting "Properties.") Just copy the address and paste it into the Blogger form. Finally, choose a layout from the options, select the size you want the picture to be, and then click "Upload Image." It will automatically appear in your post. (By the way, you can add more than one image at a time by clicking the "Add another image" link on the image upload page.)

Figure 3.4   Blogger also makes it easy to add pictures to your post.

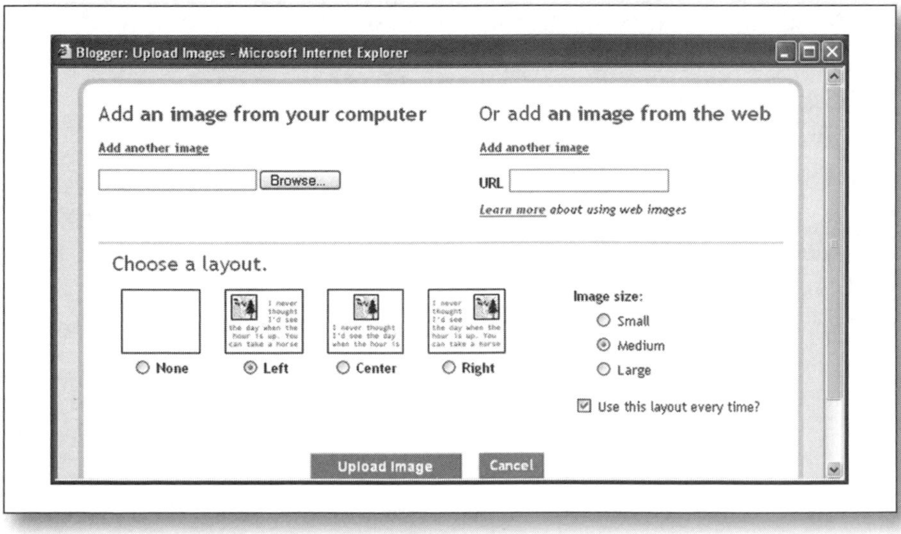

SOURCE: Used with permission of Google Inc.

Finally, you'll need to make one last adjustment to Blogger regarding safety. In the upper right-hand corner of the Blogger template, you'll see a link for "Next Blog." Unfortunately, that links to a random Weblog that might not be the most appropriate for a student to view. The good news is you can remove the button. Here's how: First, click the "Template" tab and then click the "Edit HTML" sub tab. Next, scroll down to where you see "body {." Just paste the following on a new line just above that spot:

```
#navbar-iframe {

height: 0px

visibility: hidden;

display: none

}
```

That should solve the problem.

And that's really all you need to get started with Blogger. There are other free hosting services that you might consider, but if you want more functionality and greater levels of control over what does and doesn't get posted, you'll probably have to consider using a different software program that you either pay to have hosted or host yourself. Here are a couple of noteworthy options that you might want to consider:

Edublogs.org runs on WordPress and is an open-source blog solution that has become extremely popular. In just a couple of years, Edublogs has grown to serve over 300,000 education-related blogs, and it continues to grow. WordPress gives teachers the ability to set permissions and access, and it allows them to approve work before it is published. Also, there are a lot of nice-looking templates to choose from. Again, running WordPress on your local server may require some expert technical support.

Finally, there is 21Classes.com. (Full disclosure: I consulted on this project.) 21Classes offers a free service for teachers and students (limited to 2 MB of space per site) that creates some really interesting workflows between teachers and students. It's easy for teachers to create student blogs, to monitor student activity, and to select which blog posts to publish or to keep private. As with Edublogs, there is a pay service as well that allows for more space and customizability.

For further reference, here's a Blogger's "Good Educator's Blogs" to read:

- David Warlick (tinyurl.com/j6shy)
- Clay Burrell (tinyurl.com/ytfbro)
- Chris Lehmann (tinyurl.com/62az3t)
- George Siemens (tinyurl.com/2uafn)

- Jeff Utecht (tinyurl.com/2c2ery)
- Sheryl Nussbaum-Beach (tinyurl.com/24khzy)
- Stephen Downes (tinyurl.com/164y6)
- danah boyd (tinyurl.com/zuer7)
- Tom Hoffman (tinyurl.com/225srt)
- Vicki Davis (tinyurl.com/lwwbt9)
- Shelly Blake-Plock (tinyurl.com/cz3b3f)
- Clarence Fisher (tinyurl.com/26q6vq)

And with that, you should be well on your way. As you'll see, blogs are only one of many tools of the Read/Write Web, but I would argue that they are the most important, and the most reasonable place to start your travels. No one knows what blogs may look like in five or ten years, but I can tell you that no matter what, their impact and influence on education will be felt. Welcome to the blogosphere!

4 Wikis

Easy Collaboration for All

Imagine a world in which every single person on the planet is given free access to the sum of all human knowledge. That's what we're doing.

—Jimmy Wales, Wikipedia founder

If you want to find the most important site on the Web these days, look no further than Wikipedia.org (see Figure 4.1). As its name suggests, Wikipedia is an encyclopedia, one that really is attempting to store the "sum of human knowledge." By the time you read this, the English version of Wikipedia will house over 3 million separate entries with information about everything from the Aaadonta (a type of slug) to Zzzax (a fictional super villain from Marvel Comics). Every day, new entries are being added about people, places, things, historical events, and even today's news almost as it happens. It's truly an amazing resource.

But whereas most people get the "pedia" part of the name, only a few really understand the first part, the "wiki." And believe it or not, that's the most important part, because without the wiki, this encyclopedia, this growing repository of all we know and do, could not exist. The word *wiki* is a short form of the Hawaiian *wiki-wiki,* which means "quick." Ward Cunningham created the first wiki in 1995, who was looking to design an easy authoring tool that might spur people to publish. And the key word here is "easy," because, plainly put, a wiki is a Web site where anyone can edit anything anytime they want.

So, have some knowledge about your favorite hobby that isn't on Wikipedia? Add it. Read something you think isn't correct? Fix it. Don't like the way one of the entries is written? Erase it. Something big just happen in the news that is history making? Start a new entry. You have the power, because every time you access Wikipedia, or most any other wiki for that matter, you

Figure 4.1 Wikipedia is one of the most important sites for educators to understand. It represents the potential of collaboration on the Web.

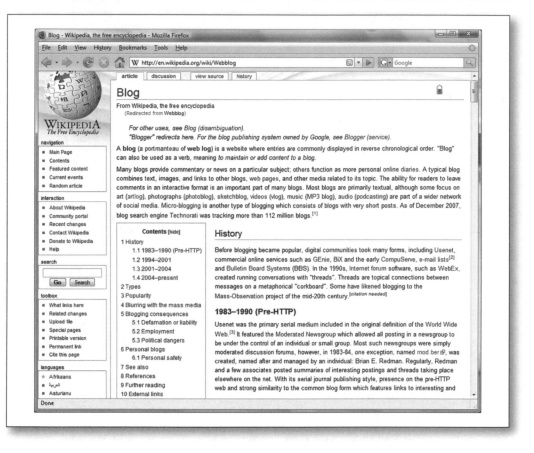

do so as editor in chief. And it's that freedom that has made Wikipedia the phenomenon it is as tens of thousands of editors in chief, people just like you and me, take on the job of collecting the sum of all human knowledge.

Most everyone's first reaction to that is that it sounds more like Whackypedia. "If anyone can edit anything on the site any time they want, how in the world can you trust what you read there?" they ask. It's a great question. The answer is that, thankfully, there are vastly more editors who want to make it right than those who want to make it wrong. When mistakes occur or vandals strike, the collaborative efforts of the group set it straight, usually very quickly. University of Buffalo professor Alex Halavais tested this by creating 13 errors on various posts on Wikipedia, all of which were fixed within a couple of hours (Halavais, 2004). Pretty amazing, I'd say.

Now, I know what you're thinking, something along the lines of "Well, I can skip this chapter, 'cause this anyone-can-do-anything wiki thing will never work in my school." But, try to resist the urge; wikis can be pretty amazing and versatile. And if you believe as I do that doing real collaboration is something that every student needs to learn, keep reading.

Take, for example, the Wikipedia entry created around the Indian Ocean earthquake that struck just after Christmas 2004 and created the tsunami that killed more than 175,000 people. It may have happened over five years ago now, but it was without question the event that made clear to me that we were living in a much different information world as I turned to Wikipedia to watch the event unfold. The earthquake occurred just after midnight (GMT) on December 26, and the first 76-word post was created at Wikipedia about nine hours later. Twenty-four hours after the first mention, the entry had been edited more than 400 times and had grown to about 3,000 words, complete with some of the first photographs of the devastation, a chart documenting the dead and injured, and other graphics describing how the tsunami was spawned.

Forty-eight hours after the first post, the entry had grown to more than 6,500 words, had been edited 1,200 times, and contained more than a dozen graphics including video of the wave itself. Six months after the event, more than 7,000 changes had been recorded, and the post had settled at around 7,200 words. All of it had been created and re-created by people just like you and me who were interested in contributing what they were finding to the entry. It was without question the most comprehensive resource on the Web about that horrific event. And that process is being repeated over and over as news happens around us. It's how each of Wikipedia's millions of entries in over 200 languages have evolved—from the hands of people just like us with the concept that everyone together is smarter than anyone alone. In the process, we check facts, provide "soft" security by acting like a community watchdog, and weed out bias and emotion from the posts in an attempt to arrive at a neutral point of view for each article. Each entry is the group's best effort, not any one person's.

In that way, Wikipedia is the poster child for the collaborative construction of knowledge and truth that the new, interactive Web facilitates. It is, to me at least, one of the main reasons I believe in the transformative potential of all of these technologies. No one person, or even small group of people, could produce Wikipedia, as currently edits appear at a rate of around 400,000 a day. Every day, thousands of people who have no connection to one another engage in the purposeful work of negotiating and creating truth. They do this with no expectation that their contributions will be in some way acknowledged or compensated, and they do it with the understanding that what they contribute can be freely edited or modified or reused by anyone else for any purpose. The extent to which this happens and to which it is successful is truly inspiring.

And the fact is that whether or not we like the concept of Wikipedia, I think we need to teach Wikipedia to our students. Why? Well, first, because they are already using it in their research, whether we like it or not. Wikipedia entries consistently come up in the top ten search results for just about anything we're looking for, and our students use it a great deal. Second, because Wikipedia is becoming a trusted and cited source by many major news outlets (the *New York Times* among them) and scholars. As well it should be. In 2007, the *Denver Post* "graded" Wikipedia by asking experts to review entries in their field of study. "Four out of five agreed their relevant Wikipedia entries are accurate, informative, comprehensive and a great resource for students" (Booth, 2007). And finally, there is much to learn in the process of using Wikipedia that can help our students become better learners—namely, collaboration and negotiation skills.

The success of Wikipedia has spawned a wiki revolution. Not only can you contribute to the sum of all human knowledge, you can add your favorite recipes to the Recipes Wiki (tinyurl.com/64q8em), your best vacation bargains to Wikitravel.org, even your favorite spots for Buffalo wings to, you guessed it, the Buffalo wings wiki (tinyurl.com/5ss9wu). There's also Wiktionary, Wikinews, Wikispecies, and Wikiquotes. You get the idea.

Like blogs, wikis are beginning to make inroads in just about every area of life. Corporations like Disney, McDonalds, Sony, and BMW have started using wikis to manage documents and information. MIT, Stanford, and other colleges and universities are testing the waters with their faculty and students. The city of Rochester, New York, is using a wiki to let people share resources, experiences, and favorite diversions (Rocwiki.org). In fact, there are now tens of thousands of wikis growing out there for just about every reason imaginable, including sites for everything from song lyrics (Lyricwiki.org) to Star Trek (Memory-alpha.org). (In fact, the Star Trek wiki is one of the most impressive out there!)

In addition, project teams are also using wikis as a way to keep track of their work, by businesses who want their employees to share information and collaborate in an easy way, and teachers who want to collaboratively build resource sites for their classes. (Much more about that in a minute.) There are now even password-protected wikis that allow people to use the technology behind closed doors, and there are over 100 different wiki programs, most of them free via open source, which you can install on your server. In other words, just like blogs, wikis are coming of age.

So, how exactly do wikis work? Every page in a wiki has a link, usually at the top, which says "Edit Page" or something similar. When you click it, it either takes you to the code behind the page or to a WYSIWYG (What You See Is What You Get) editor, depending on the software you are using. At that point, you just begin making your edits. Simple as that.

Each page on a wiki also comes with another very important feature: a page history. The link to it is usually near the "Edit Page" link, and when you click it you can see when changes were made, by whom, and what was changed. The best part is that, if need be, you can easily use the history list to revert back to a previous version of the page should someone come and muck things up. This, in fact, is how most vandalism is dealt with, and what makes vandals give up. And from a technical aspect, that's pretty much all you need to know.

But one tab that not a lot of people really understand is the "Discussion" tab. While wikis are not as good as blogs at carrying on a conversation about ideas, the Discussion tab allows editors or contributors to carry out the negotiation over what should appear in the entry being created. To get a feel for this, take a look at the conversation going on behind the entry on global warming at Wikipedia (tinyurl.com/33885n). Not only will you learn a lot about the efforts of the contributors to "get it right," you'll also get a sense of the types of give-and-take skills that will serve our students well in the future. It's real collaboration made transparent.

Philosophically, wikis can play havoc with the traditional ideas of copyright and intellectual property. Obviously, they follow closely the open-source software ideal that the quality of the collectively produced product is more important than owning the idea or the code. Really, wikis bring the concept of open source to the mainstream, as the ideas and process are no longer reserved just for software developers.

All of these challenges are great entry points for a discussion about the use of wikis in the classroom. As we continue to move toward a world where everyone has access to ideas and where collaboration is the expectation rather than the exception, wikis can go a long way toward teaching our students some very useful skills for their future.

THE CHALLENGE OF WIKIPEDIA IN SCHOOLS

Before we talk about building our own wikis with students, a couple of more thoughts on Wikipedia. Already, students are turning to Wikipedia as a resource for research, much to the chagrin of many teachers and librarians. As we've already discussed with blogs, knowing what sources to trust is becoming a much more labor-intensive exercise, and wikis, with many often anonymous authors, make that even more difficult. The idea that "it might be wrong" is a tough one for most people to overcome. Yet Steve Jobs, the CEO of Apple, has called Wikipedia one of the most accurate encyclopedias in the world (tinyurl.com/33uqlh). What to do?

For one, teachers should spend some time checking Wikipedia's accuracy on their own. If your experience is anything like mine has been, you may end up agreeing with Jobs. But this still takes a faith that we didn't need in the days before the interactive Web, a faith that collectively we can produce information that is as high quality as what a trusted few produced in the past. It's a tough call. The early consensus among educators seems to be to tell students to use Wikipedia as a starting point for their work, but not as a sole resource.

The additional challenge with Wikipedia is that each of its entries is, in fact, a collaboratively written research report. It's not exposition in the sense that the entries are defending a thesis—just the opposite, in fact. Wikipedia's whole intention is to foster a neutral point of view in every entry. But say you assign students to do reports on a specific country—Argentina, for instance. All the pertinent reporting about Argentina may have already been done and collected at Wikipedia. So in this case, is it more important for a student to be able to find that information and know how to evaluate it, or to know how to repeat work that's already been done? Again, it's a tough call.

A final challenge is changing the way we think about the content our own students create. Should we be encouraging them to contribute what they learn and know to the Wikipedia entry on that topic? Think about it. If your student produces a great research paper on global warming, why shouldn't she add what she found to the global warming entry at Wikipedia? And why shouldn't we watch together to see what happens to that information that she adds? If it gets modified, we can think critically about those modifications. If it gets spammed (which is highly unlikely) we can come to the rescue. Either way, it can be a great learning experience. (And by the way, for younger kids, they could edit or add their work to Simple English Wikipedia at Simple.Wikipedia.org.)

If we begin to look at Wikipedia as another opportunity for our students to contribute what they learn and know to a larger audience, I think we can begin to appreciate it for the really incredible site that it is.

WIKIS IN SCHOOLS

So what about it? Are you ready to begin thinking about how a wiki might work in your classroom? Hopefully, despite the seemingly chaotic design of wikis, you're starting to imagine the possibilities here. So, before taking a look at the ways in which some forward-thinking teachers have been using wikis in their classrooms, let's talk about some of the more obvious concerns. Namely, what would stop someone from anonymously going onto a class-run wiki and vandalizing it by erasing content or by adding profanities, for instance? There is no doubt that teachers on the K–12 levels are going to be hard pressed to justify the use of such an open venue for the publication of student work. However, as we'll see, there are some who are doing just that. In theory, the "soft security" model could work in schools as well. If it's used as a group collaboration site à la Wikipedia, the class as a whole could monitor the content that is added and make the necessary edits and revisions. Giving students editorial control can imbue in them a sense of responsibility and ownership for the site and minimize the risk of someone adding something offensive. In fact, wiki projects in schools have worked best when the teacher loosens the reins a bit and lets students manage the content on the site.

As much as we'd like to trust our students to make good things happen, however, we all know that it would only take one parent to open the wiki and find something inappropriate to derail the project. The good news is that there are alternatives. Although wiki purists scoff at the idea, there are a number of Web-based wiki sites that feature a password and login system similar to Weblogs for people to interact with the site. Or, similar software can be installed on your server and run locally. It's still a much more open and collaborative environment once inside, but in this way you can restrict who can and cannot access the site.

Wikis pose some pedagogical challenges as well. They can be so effective at fostering collaboration that the teacher really needs to carefully examine her role in their use. As I noted previously, early implementations of wikis in educational settings have shown that the more autonomy teachers give to students in terms of negotiating the scope and quality of the content they are creating, the better. It's a very democratic process of knowledge creation. In using wikis, students are not only learning how to publish content; they are also learning how to develop and use all sorts of collaborative skills, negotiating with others to agree on correctness, meaning, relevance, and more. In essence, students begin to teach each other. Teachers who impose a lot of right and wrong on that process can undermine the effectiveness of the tool. (For further discussion of the pedagogical potentials see tinyurl.com/2zu6fb.)

And remember, if the openness of wikis feels a bit too disruptive, wikis can be used in many other contexts inside schools as well. As we'll see, they can be used as collaborative tools among teachers or districts to collect and share information.

So how might we use wikis in our classrooms? One of the most obvious ways is to create an online text for your curriculum that you and your students can both contribute to. A co-construction of this type could make for a much more personalized text, one specific to your particular class. Or, consider adding other students and other teachers who teach the same class. It could easily become a resource, a showcase for best practices, and an articulation tool as well. Students might use it to create their own class Wikipedia. If it's a physics class, for instance, students could post and edit entries that deal with the structure of the atom or ionization or . . . other things.

(Remember, I was an English teacher.) They could add graphics and links, annotations and reflections. Just like blogs, they could also post PowerPoint presentations, video and audio files, and spreadsheets. And all of those collectively assembled artifacts could serve as a starting point for future classes to then edit and add to.

Personally, the ability to easily amass and publish a wide-ranging, tailor-made resource like this is why I have a feeling that textbook manufacturers don't like the ideas of wikis one bit. Sure, they can always say that you can't trust a source that's not professionally edited. But in the era of the Read/Write Web, we are all editors, and we must all become skilled at doing that work. As these tools become more and more accessible, and as they continue to foster the publication and sharing of reliable information, it may not be long until traditional textbooks will fade into the background.

This is already happening on a wide scale at Wikibooks (see Figure 4.2), where almost 40,000 pages of textbook materials have been created in five years (tinyurl.com/9nsoq). This brings up another way that you can use wikis in your classroom: Have your students create or edit entries to books that have already been started elsewhere. Introduce them to the concept of a wiki,

Figure 4.2   Wikibooks is a site that hosts all sorts of collaboratively written texts.

show them how it works, have them pick an entry to edit, review their edits with them, have them share the link when their work is posted, and then have them track their edits to see how others might edit them. Wikijunior, an off-shoot of Wikibooks, may be just the ticket (tinyurl.com/ma7hw). Wikijunior is in the process of producing a series of full-color booklets for children age eight to eleven, and it is in need of your students' contributions. It's a great opportunity to introduce students to the concepts of open-source software, community collaboration, respect for other people's ideas, intellectual property and public domain, and much more.

EXAMPLES OF WIKIS IN K–12 EDUCATION

Among the teachers using wikis in schools, few have done more than Vicki Davis at Westwood High in Camilla, Georgia. Her computer classes use the Westwood.Wikispaces.com site to complete many of their projects and as a portal for assignments and relevant links to many other sources. But even more, Vicki has started to use wikis to connect her students to other learners from around the world, and her "Flat Classroom" project wiki from 2007 (flatclassroomproject.wikispaces.com) and her Horizon Project from 2008 (tinyurl.com/2knznm) are great examples.

The first title comes from Thomas Friedman's *The World Is Flat* and the idea was to have her students study some of the "flatteners" that Friedman describes in terms of how they play out not only in their local lives in Georgia but for students in other parts of the globe. So she connected with Julie Lindsay, a teacher then in Bangladesh, and together they connected their students for a two-week investigation, the results of which are reported in the wiki. As you dig through the site, you'll find a comprehensive collection of narratives and essays, audio, and video—all produced collaboratively by teams of kids from disparate geographies. It's really good stuff.

And when you see it, you'll also see why a wiki makes perfect sense for delivering this kind of work. The students worked together in the same environment. They could edit and add to each other's work seamlessly. The pages were easy to build and grow. And best of all, it's an environment that is easy to share with large audiences. Pretty cool.

Or, take a look at Louise Maine's wiki work at her school in Punxsutawney, Pennsylvania. She and her freshman biology students are tracking their work from class, sharing links, posting results to experiments, and basically building a text for their course (tinyurl.com/nr91yr). More importantly, her students are learning the literacies of collaboratively constructing content as they work with her to add value to the site. While only her students can edit it, the wiki is open for anyone in the world to view.

Another great wiki-using teacher is Jason Welker at the Zurich International School. His Welker's Wikinomics site is one of the most beautifully designed class wikis out there (shown in Figure 4.3, tinyurl.com/6ruy3y). And it is an amazing example of what collaborative construction by students can produce.

Figure 4.3   Jason Welker at the Zurich International School uses a WetPaint wiki for his AP Economics course. His students use the wiki to create a year-long study guide for the AP exam.

Jason's AP Economics students are writing and continually editing a comprehensive review text for the AP exam. Under the "Course Information" section in the left-hand column, you will see links to the entire course syllabus, as well as links to the individual pages that he and his students are creating under the micro- and macroeconomics sections. Each unit has several subchapters where students enter whatever information and resources they feel will help them in their preparation.

In addition, Jason's students post podcasts of their work and thinking, and viewers can take in relevant YouTube videos students have found. As with most wiki sites these days, they have embedded a chat box that any one of them can use to connect when they are on the site, both with each other and Jason, and they are carrying on discussions about everything from "The shortcomings of GDP" to "Is there a limit to economic expansion?"

One interesting aspect of the wiki software that Jason uses, WetPaint, is that it is easy to track the participation of his students. It's easy to access statistics on each user that not only tally how many times he or she edited but also make plain what those edits were. (See tinyurl.com/ys7kd6 for an example.)

Importantly, the class wiki has a link back to the class blog where class members are posting outside reading on a regular basis. It's a great example of how to begin to integrate some of these different tools into an online learning ecology where students are doing meaningful work for real purposes.

Or how about doing a book study on a wiki? That's what Georgia teacher Shelley Paul did when her students read *Turn Homeward, Hannalee* by Patricia Beatty (tinyurl.com/36sy57). The class wiki has all sorts of student-created content that gives context to the work, everything from interviews with storytellers, to presentations about local mills that are similar to those in the story, to all sorts of reference pages that explain parts of the text. The whole site provides a great deal of information that others can use in the study of the book. And that's just what has happened. In the first six months the wiki has been visited about 13,000 times from readers across the globe. Shelley says, "Collaborating on the *Hannalee* project was one of the most rewarding teaching experiences I have ever had. Students instinctively invested in the idea that the project was an evolution—that it could always be made better, and that it was the collaboration that made it such a worthy resource—some tremendously important learning concepts that I don't think traditional schooling addresses very effectively. Our biggest "problem" is that these students now expect to do similarly meaningful work for every book they study!" (S. Paul, personal communication, June 15, 2007).

And then there is PlanetMath.com (tinyurl.com/90rxf), "a virtual community that aims to help make mathematical knowledge more accessible." This is a dynamic community of math educators that is collaboratively creating a mathematics encyclopedia (à la Wikipedia), and anyone can participate. (Just sign up to become a member.) Currently there are over 8,500 entries, ranging from abelian to Zuckerman's Number, neither of which I remember studying in school. In this case, each entry has an "owner" that reviews any changes on a regular basis, but the concept is the same.

One last favorite wiki of mine comes from students at Mercy Vocational High School in Philadelphia, who have been making annual trips to the towns devastated by Hurricane Katrina. Last year was their fourth such excursion, and they decided to use a wiki to document their travel, their work, and their learning. Their "Operation Katrina 2009" site (tinyurl.com/c62ja2) is at once a diary, photo album, and video record that allows parents and community members (and other readers from around the world) to share in the experience. It's a great use of a wiki site to chronicle and archive all of the good work those students are doing.

So let's take a minute and imagine the possibilities here. Your students, with just a little help from you, could create book-report wikis, "what-I-did-this-summer" wikis, brainstorming wikis, poetry wikis, notes-from-class wikis, sixth-grade wikis, history-of-the-school or -community wikis, formula wikis, wikis for individual countries they might be studying, political-party wikis, exercise wikis . . . you get the idea. And you could create similar spaces for colleagues to save research or do articulation or much, much more. Whatever topic might lend itself to the collaborative collection of content relating to its study, a wiki is a great choice.

WIKI TOOLS FOR SCHOOLS

If you want to give wikis a try in your classroom, you may want to start at the Wikispaces.com site shown in Figure 4.4. (After playing here for a bit to get your feet wet, you may want to think about trying Wetpaint.com as well.) At this writing, they have given away over 180,000 ad-free wikis to educators, and you can follow this link to get your own: tinyurl.com/293h9a. As you can tell from most of the examples above, Wikispaces is already pretty popular with classroom teachers, though there are some alternatives we'll discuss later.

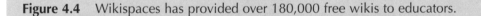

Figure 4.4 Wikispaces has provided over 180,000 free wikis to educators.

Creating your wiki is as easy as filling in the form on the page linked above, a process that takes maybe 45 seconds if you're a fast typist. (A minute if not.) Enter a username, a password, and a working e-mail address, click the "yes" button to make a wiki, give your wiki a name (no spaces allowed, by the way), select the type of wiki you want (most educators pick "protected" to start), click the box to certify that you're using it for educational purposes, and you're up and running. All you need to do is click the "Edit This Page" icon when your wiki site appears and you can start creating the content on your site.

Using the editing toolbar, you can do some basic formatting of your text, but even better you can easily add audio and even video to your page. (You can even add a Google Calendar if you like—very cool.) Just click on the little TV-looking icon and follow the instructions on the dialog box that pops up. And, you can easily upload files or pictures up to 20 MB in size from your computer right onto the page. Use the picture icon to do that. When you're all done, just save the page and then view the result. If you don't like it, click "Edit This Page" and have at it again.

Now, one of the most important aspects of building wikis is the ability to easily add subpages and layers to your site. Wikispaces makes this very easy. Say you want to create a separate page for your students to collaborate on a skateboarding essay. And, you want that essay linked from the front page of your site. All you need to do is type the words "Skateboarding Essay" somewhere on the page, highlight it, and then click the link icon on the toolbar. In the dialog box that pops up, you'll see the highlighted text in the "Link Text" line, and then you'll also see it listed in the "New Page Name" line. Just click "OK," then save the page, then click on the linked "Skateboarding Essay" that shows up. It will take you to a new page where all you (or your students) have to do is—you guessed it—click on "Edit This Page." (Remember, when you want to create a link to another Web page, choose the "external link" tab from the pop-up box that appears when you click the link icon.)

Wikispaces also has the "Discussion" tab where you and your students can add reflections on the work or negotiate what should or shouldn't be on the page. It's a great way of making the process of content creation transparent. And, as all good wikis do, there is also a "History" tab where you can view all of the changes to any page and who made them.

Now, one important step to making sure you can track who is doing what in Wikispaces is to have separate accounts for each student you want editing your wiki. Wikispaces makes this pretty easy. When you are logged in, click on the "Manage Wiki" link, and then click on the icon labeled "User Creator." There you can actually upload a spreadsheet with all of your student info that you can then easily turn into individual accounts. By doing this, students will be able to log into the site when they edit, and you can be pretty sure who is doing what to the site when you check the history. (Remember, nothing is 100 percent certain.)

Lots of teachers also like PBwiki (PBwiki.com), which is almost as easy to use, and once you get the hang of the wiki world, you might want to test drive Google's wiki tool called "Sites." (When you are logged into the Google account you created for Blogger, just go to Sites.Google.com.) And, like I said earlier, Wetpaint.com is another popular wiki tool that may be worth your time to explore more fully.

OTHER WIKI TOOLS AND RESOURCES

As I said before, there are a whole slew of different wiki programs that you can choose from if Wikispaces or PBwiki don't fit the bill. The best list that I've found is the Wiki Engines list at tinyurl.com/34584q. (Note: You may want to visit the site with whoever runs your servers.)

Finally, there are a few other interesting and cool wiki-type tools I'll mention that you might want to take a look at. First, there is Webnote, which is like an online Post-it note repository (tinyurl.com/4w8eo). Basically, you go to the site, create a page name in the form, and click "Load" to get started. You can add a Post-it by clicking the little yellow icon in the upper left and then double-clicking in the yellow Post-it-type box that appears. You can include basic HTML inside the boxes, and you can color code your notes for easy sorting. All of your notes are totally searchable, so you might want to think about creating some standard tag words to add as you go along.

But the coolest thing about Webnote is that you can easily save snippets of text from Web pages you might be visiting. Here's how: The first time you go to your notes page, type "B" and a note will appear with a link for a book-marklet. Drag the link to your "Links" toolbar on your browser, and the next time you're visiting a page and you find some text you want to save to your Webnote page, just highlight it and click that link. Automatically, you'll be taken to your note page and you'll see your highlighted text in a box with a link to the source. Cool, huh? If you want to edit that note, just double-click it.

Now why is this a wiki? Because anyone who knows where your page is can come in and add, edit, or delete notes. That's right. Anyone. Good news is that makes it easy to share the space. Bad news is, well, you know the risks by now. But again, if someone comes in and destroys the content on the page, you can always revert back to the last correct version. So, although Webnote may be a bit too open for student use, you could create a Webnote page for group study or research with other teachers, and you can even subscribe to the RSS feed for that page to monitor what they are posting.

And then there is Google's other offering at Google Docs (Docs.Google.com). While aimed more at being a free alternative to programs like Word and Excel, they also have wiki-esque features in that you can invite anyone to edit and create the document or table, and you have a history of who has done what in terms of changes. And, like all the rest, you can publish your work to the world at large in just one click. Google Sites, their full-fledged wiki tool, is also an option worth checking out.

Regardless of how educators feel about the potential of wikis, and I can understand the hesitancy many teachers feel, one thing remains certain: The collaborative environment that wikis facilitate can teach students much about how to work with others, how to create community, and how to operate in a world where the creation of knowledge and information is more and more becoming a group effort. I'm serious when I say that I get chills sometimes when I think about the amazing work that's being done at Wikipedia. In many ways, it gives me great hope for the future because it is a testament, I think, of good people doing good. Using wikis, we can start to show our students what it means to be a part of that process.

And if the wiki bug does bite you as it has me, this might come in handy:

> *Please grant me the serenity to accept the pages I cannot edit,*
>
> *The courage to edit the pages I can,*
>
> *And the wisdom to know the difference*
>
> —The Wiki Prayer
> (tinyurl.com/2t8fdf)

Have fun!

5 RSS

The New Killer App for Educators

True or false: Weblogs and wikis and their friends (which we'll get to later) are creating so much more content on the Web that there's just no way to keep track of it and find the relevant stuff you need to know.

If you said true, you're half right. (Which, of course, means you're half right if you said false, too.) The ability of average Joes and Janes to easily publish content to the Internet certainly is creating an avalanche of information that feels absolutely overwhelming. But the good news is that the tools of the Read/Write Web are not just focused on publishing. There are also a few tools aimed at helping you consume all that information in more efficient and relevant ways. Meet RSS.

RSS stands for Really Simple Syndication, and if you're an educator, I think it's the one technology that you should start using today, right now, this minute. And tomorrow, you should teach your students to use it.

In simple terms, Weblogs (and an ever-growing number of other sites) generate a behind-the-scenes code in a language similar to HTML called XML. This code, usually referred to as a "feed," as in "news feed," makes it possible for readers to "subscribe" to the content that is created on a particular Weblog so they no longer have to visit the blog itself to get it. As is true with traditional syndication, the content comes to you instead of you going to get it, hence "Really Simple Syndication."

For instance, say you're a political science teacher and you've found 20 or 30 Weblog and media sites on the Internet that are consistently publishing interesting and relevant information for you and your students. Finding the time to click through to those sites and keep abreast of any new information on a regular basis would be nearly impossible. But what if you only had to go to one place to read all of the new content on all of those sites?

Wouldn't be so difficult, would it? Well, that's exactly what RSS feeds allow you to do by using a type of software called an "aggregator" or feed collector. The aggregator checks the feeds you subscribe to, usually every hour, and it collects all the new content from those sites you are subscribed to. Then, when you're ready, you open up your aggregator to read the individual stories, file them for later use, click through to the site itself, or delete them if they're not relevant. In other words, you check one site instead of thirty—not a bad trade-off for a typically harried teacher.

Here's another scenario: You currently get the headlines from the *New York Times* via an e-mail message that arrives each morning. But more and more, spammers selling everything from pornography to mortgages are clogging up your e-mail box. There are new virus warnings every day. That *New York Times* content is getting lost in the morass that e-mail has become. Not so with RSS. the *New York Times,* as well as hundreds of other newspapers, magazines, television stations, and the like, has a number of virus-free "feeds" that your aggregator can collect. (If they don't have what you want, you can create your own.) And, in general, you know that everything in your aggregator is something you want to read because you subscribed to it. No ads, no spam—just new content from the sources you read.

So, reason number one to get your brain wrapped around RSS? You can read more content from more sources in less time. In fact, you may even be able to cancel the subscriptions you have to paper versions of magazines and newspapers that come to your nondigital mailbox. With RSS, you can create your own collections of news and features that are personalized to your interests—what some people are calling "The Daily Me."

But there is an even better reason, I think, to use RSS. Not only can you have the news and ideas of the day come to your aggregator, you can also use RSS to let you know when someone out there on the Web has published something with certain keywords that you might be interested in. So, by using RSS, you can create a feed for "global warming New Jersey" that will bring new results as they are published right to your online mailbox.

Now think for a second about what that means. Students can be immediately updated when new information about research topics is published. Teachers could track the blogosphere for discussions about motivating students or the unique pedagogies of the class. Superintendents could be notified about what's being written about their schools. Once again, the possibilities are, well, pretty interesting.

RSS is a technology that will change your life, if you let it. Over the last few years, it has become one of the building blocks for the personal learning curriculum I've constructed for myself. I've been able to track about 80 feeds of information daily, from bloggers, newspapers, search engines, and more. Over that time, I have read or skimmed literally tens of thousands of posts and developed a fairly keen eye for quickly spotting the most relevant and interesting information. And this is another one of those skills that our students, the knowledge workers of the future, are going to have to develop in order to flourish. Given the fact that the amount of information going online shows no sign of slowing, if they are unable to consistently collect potentially relevant information for their lives and careers and quickly discern what of that information is most useful, they will be at a disadvantage. And the National Council of Teachers of English (NCTE) knows this too. One of their new "Twenty-First Century Literacies" is that "twenty-first century readers and writers need to manage, analyze, and synthesize multiple streams of simultaneous information" (NCTE, 2008). RSS is a perfect tool for this. And, as with the rest of these changes, it's our job to model and teach these skills.

So, we're going to cover a lot of ground in the next few pages, but before we do, a bit of advice: Go slowly. If you really want to understand the potential of RSS, take a week or two to work through the techniques in this chapter. None of them are particularly difficult, I promise. But the results can be a bit overwhelming. Don't be surprised if at first you think RSS is adding to your information overload instead of easing it. With a little time and experience, you'll begin to understand why pretty soon RSS will be a household tool, and why it will make you and your students smarter, more effective consumers of information.

SETTING UP AN RSS FEED READER

Ready to start? First, you need to set up a mailbox or an "aggregator" to collect your RSS feeds. While there are a number of pretty good online aggregators to select from, I would suggest Google Reader. Why? It's free, easy, and it includes a whole host of ways that you can begin publishing and connecting the news and information it collects. While there are a number of great downloadable aggregators out there that can do wonderful things, the main advantage to Google Reader is that you can access it from anywhere you have an Internet connection. In other words, you don't have to be on your own computer(s) with special software installed to read your news. (For a full list of aggregators you might choose from, check out "News on Feeds" at tinyurl.com/2x7zhs.)

If you already took the time to set up a Google account for Blogger, then you already have a Reader account just waiting for you to start playing with. If you go to Google.com/reader when you are logged in, it should appear. If you didn't set up a Google account, what on earth are you waiting for? Like it or not, Google has all sorts of tools that educators can put to good use.

The thing that made me move to Reader from another great online aggregator at Bloglines.com a couple of years ago is that it's almost too easy to begin subscribing to feeds with Reader. So let's get started. While getting your RSS feet wet, it's best to focus on one topic that you want to start building your reading around. So, what's your passion? Astrophysics? Schnauzers? Frisbee Golf? Whatever it might be, just click on the "Add Subscription" link at the top left of the page and type the word or words into the form that pops up. Reader will then display some of the feeds out there on the Web that are about your passion. So, for instance, for you dog lovers out there, you can subscribe to blogs like "Life with Schnauzers" or the "Schnauzer World Web Ring" or "Anything Schnauzer." (What a world, huh?) All you need to do is click on the "Subscribe" button below the title and more schnauzer news than you can shake a bone at will start filling up your aggregator.

Now, before we get too far into the adding subscriptions process, I want to take a few minutes to talk about the importance of making sure the sites you add are worthwhile. This is a part of digital reading literacy that our students will have to master, a vetting process that they (and we) should be going through whenever we land on a new site on the Web. While each of us will have a different process for this, I do think there are some basic starting points for assessing the veracity of any Web page and the value of any potential RSS feed you might subscribe to. They are, in no particular order:

- Are there advertisements? While ads don't disqualify a site, they do reveal something about the agenda of the site owner.
- Is the author's full name used? I tend to trust bloggers who use their full names more than anonymous authors. It also gives me the opportunity to see if I can find out more about them through a Google search.
- What are the authors' (and the blogs') credentials, both traditional and nontraditional? I might do a Technorati search to get a sense of the blog's rank or search Google for links back to the site. (Just put "link:" in front of the site's address with no spaces, for example, "link:weblogg-ed.com.")
- How often is the site updated? Obviously, if you're thinking of subscribing, there should be a consistent flow of information.
- What is the quality of the writing? Is it measured or overly opinionated, easy to read, relevant, and so on?

Are there comments? Well-established conversations and communities lend themselves to better reading and potential network building. But it's not just the frequency of the comments—the quality of the comments is just as important.

Okay, back to our searching. So what if your search terms didn't net you anything worthwhile? Then what? Well, Reader will actually help you find RSS feeds at your favorite sites if they are available. For instance, just click on "Add Subscription" and type in "NASA". When you click "Add," you'll see all sorts of feeds that the space agency provides. If NASA isn't your passion, just put in any Web site address that you visit often and Reader will see what's available. Or just paste in the address of those blogs you read regularly (like Weblogg-ed.com). Remember, however, not every site on the Web has an RSS feed. Also, for a ready-made list of feeds from governments from around the world, schools and universities, businesses, and many more, try the RSS Compendium (tinyurl.com/olf7t).

Another way you can find feeds is to search for them in a standard Web search. For instance, say you want to see if your local paper or favorite magazine has any feeds you can subscribe to. Just search for the title of the publication and the letters RSS (as in "'New York Times' RSS" or "'Cat Fancy' RSS.") When you get to the page where the feeds are listed (usually in little orange icons with the letters "RSS" or "XML" or a radio symbol) just right-click on the icon and copy the link or shortcut in the menu. Then, go back to Google Reader and paste that feed address into your "Add Subscription" line.

And really the best way to find other great teachers and sources of information to subscribe to is to simply read and follow the links in the sources you find interesting or relevant. This is all about creating networks and connections, and most bloggers I read are always pointing to other founts of knowledge that are probably in their own aggregators already. In this way, links are recommendations.

However you do it, once you have subscribed to a feed in Reader, the feed name will appear in the list on the left hand side of the page. Anytime the name is bold with a number after it, this means there is new content coming from that source that you haven't read yet. When you click on the name, the content appears on the right side of the page (see Figure 5.1). Remember, if you ever want to unsubscribe from a feed, just display it by clicking on it in the list and then choose "Unsubscribe" from the "Feed Settings" drop-down list at the top right.

Another important aspect of subscribing to RSS feeds is to make sure you come up with an organizational scheme that works for you. To do that, create new folders as you start adding various topics to your aggregator. For instance, I have a folder for "Education," another for "Culture," another for "Technology" and so on. Folders are easily created in that "Feed Settings" dropdown list as well.

So take a little time to get comfortable with the basic subscribing and managing functions of readers before you go on. And, just a suggestion, you may want to stop at about ten feeds so you don't get overwhelmed before you get practiced at reading in your aggregator. Get into the habit of checking your aggregator on a daily basis before moving into the more nuanced yet powerful uses of Reader.

Figure 5.1   Google Reader offers a clean and intuitive interface for scanning and reading your RSS feeds.

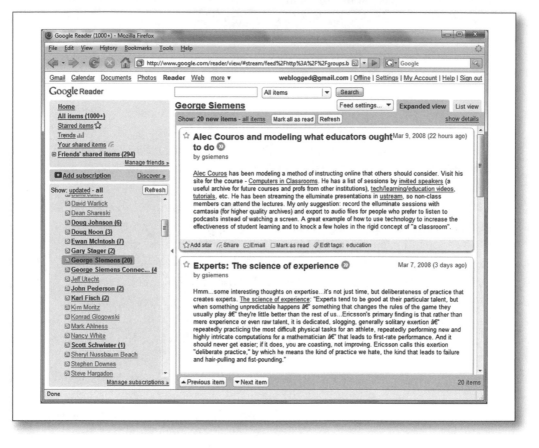

READING AND SHARING

So now that you've gotten the RSS bug, it's time to explore further what you can do with Reader and with RSS feeds in general. And there is a lot.

First, as you read the individual posts of information that come through your aggregator, you can begin to organize those that you find most relevant for later retrieval. (You may also want to do this using social bookmarks, which we'll discuss in the next chapter.) For each post, you have the ability to add your own personal "tags" or keywords that identify what that piece of content means to you. At the bottom right of each post is a link that says "Edit Tags." When you click it, you can type in as many keywords as you like. For instance, if I was reading a post on using Lulu.com to self-publish student books, I might tag it with the words "publishing, tools, fund-raiser, English101." (Single words work best, so you may have to mash together some multiword tags as in the last example.) For every tag you use, Reader creates a separate folder where it will collect all of the posts that you tag with a specific word. Your folder list will grow at the bottom of your subscription list.

While in a perfect world you would be able to read every word of every post in your aggregator and soak up the learning, many times you may just have time to scan what's in there and save the good stuff for more close reading later (see Figure 5.1). To do that, just "Add a Star" to the post you want to call up later by clicking the "Starred Posts" link at the top left of your Reader page.

And, finally, Reader has a pretty cool option that lets you create your own bloggy page of items that you find most interesting so other people on the Web can read those items too. Just click the "Share" link under any post and it will automatically show up on your public page. Click on the "Shared Items" link at the top right to get the address of that page, and then you can let other people know it's there. And yes, in case you were wondering, people can subscribe to that page using RSS. (Have I mentioned I love this stuff?)

Now, one last thing about Reader before we move on to the more specific uses of RSS. If you want to keep up with your RSS feeds but you know you won't have online access for a spell (taking a plane ride or heading out for a camping trip, let's say) you can now take your feeds with you. You'll need to download and install Google Gears (tinyurl.com/2jfv5q), which will allow you to save the text of whatever is waiting to be read in your Reader onto your laptop for later reading, online or off. The best part is you can still star or share or edit tags as you go, and when you get back online, Gears will synch up all of your actions.

USING RSS FEEDS IN THE CLASSROOM

So, you've got your favorite Weblog and media feeds in your aggregator, and you're starting to get the hang of this "getting the good stuff when I want it" concept. That means it's time to start thinking about how you might bring RSS into your school and classroom. And I think that's an important step to make at some point. As David Parry of the University of Albany writes, "The speed of reading in the age of the digital has changed, and we need to help students navigate this" (Perry, 2006). Reading literacy can no longer be how well students can decipher text on a page or screen. We have to begin to prepare them for this much more complex world. And just to drive that point home, here is a great snip from Manitoba teacher Clarence Fisher's blog:

> An aggregator is like a personal information filter. Without it the Web is a big and scary place. Having a well-stocked, well-fed aggregator is like having a personal guide. As a teacher, I consider one of my main jobs to be serving as a personal guide, helping kids

to fill their aggregators with content that is relevant and useful for them. They also need to learn most importantly to separate signal from noise. (Fisher, 2007)

In other words, there is much to be learned from RSS.

So, how can you start using this in your school and in your classroom? Well, there are a number of different ways that RSS feeds can add to your knowledge base, help you communicate, and make your teaching better.

RSS Feeds With Student Weblogs

If you already use Weblogs with your students, the uses of RSS should be pretty apparent. Instead of checking out all 25 (or 30, or more) student Weblogs every day, you could just collect their work in your aggregator using their RSS feeds. That way, you can scan through all of the class content in one place, make sure it's all appropriate, and click through to a particular post if you want to comment on it. My use of student feeds in this way drastically reduced my reading time and allowed me to make all of my classes paperless. In addition, you can provide individual student Weblog feeds to parents or counselors or whoever else might be interested in that student's work and be savvy enough to know about RSS. (Don't worry, pretty soon most people will know.)

With some Weblog packages, you can even subscribe to feeds that show new comments on the various sites, or even to just certain topics. In other words, you can track just about everything going on in your students' blogs using RSS.

In addition, Weblog software like WordPress and Blogger allow you to import RSS feeds into pages you create for your or your students' sites. While it takes a little bit of code to make it work, the benefit of bringing topic-specific feeds right into student (or teacher) work spaces is something that you might want to explore. (See also the "Including RSS Feeds in Your Weblog" later in this chapter.)

RSS Feeds Without Student Weblogs

Even if your students don't have Weblogs, you may want to have them set up their own Google Reader account. With more and more news sources producing feeds for aggregation, the breadth of current events and even topic-specific research that students could collect could go a long way in assisting them with research or further study. (It's one reason why I think RSS could be a great help for the media- and information-literacy skills students lack.) And, if you use a Weblog, they can include your feed in their aggregator to stay abreast of what is going on in class.

RSS Search Feeds

The idea of creating RSS feeds for search terms is especially interesting. Say you have a student who is doing a project or a paper on the avian flu. That student could actually create an RSS feed that would bring any news about the disease to his aggregator as soon as it was published—kind of like doing research 24/7, only the RSS feed does all the work. And, you can create a feed about any topic you want. The next section explains how.

RSS Feeds for News Searches

Both Google News and Yahoo News make it possible to track standing searches with RSS feeds. And they've both made it very easy.

Let's start with Google. Just go to News.Google.com and click the "Advanced Search" link above and to the right of the search form. Here you can add the words you want to search for, the location you want them from, and even a particular publication. (Google has about 4,500 news sources that you can choose from, and while Google does not publish this list, you can find a growing list of Google's sources at tinyurl.com/cshk7m.) Click the "Google Search" button and see what you get. If the results aren't really what you were looking for, you may need to modify your search.

If, however, the page of results looks pretty relevant, all you need to do is copy the address of that news search and go into your Google Reader account and paste the address into the "Add Subscription" form. From that point on, any time there is something in the news about the topic you searched for, the result will show up in your aggregator. And remember, you can create as many of these feeds as you like. If you ever want to stop receiving the feed, just delete it from your aggregator. (If only we could do that with spam, right?)

Remember, you may want to narrow your search to one particular news outlet by using the "Advanced Search" page, which is linked next to the search box. That way, instead of getting 500 hits a day on avian flu from around the world, you'll only get the five to ten a week from, say, the *New York Times*. Remember, however, that in a world where we have access to global resources, it's a good idea to set up searches from a few different outlets.

Okay, say you're not a Google lover and would rather use Yahoo News instead. It's just as easy. Just go to tinyurl.com/nlp, put in your search terms, and copy and paste the address into your Google Reader. In fact, Yahoo has some amazing tweaks to this process that will let you limit the region the news comes from, the language, and even category. Basically, any parameter you want to enter in an advanced search can be saved to an RSS feed. To me, that's pretty amazing. See the Yahoo Search Blog for more details (tinyurl.com/24rywx).

RSS Feeds for Weblog Searches

Getting a regular feed of searches in the blogosphere is just as easy, but you need to remember that the results aren't always going to be as, shall we say, appropriate. Obviously, the vast majority of Weblogs are not edited for content by anyone other than the author, and invariably there will be some questionable posts that will land in your aggregator. Still, Weblogs offer some really great potential research, and you might want to experiment with searching them on your own before bringing students into the fray. To do so, the easiest way is to go to Blogsearch.Google.com and type in your search terms. You should know what to do by now.

Another option is Technorati.com, which is a leader in indexing Weblog content. Once you've signed up for a free membership, you can create what Technorati calls "Watchlists." Each watchlist you create has its own RSS feed that you can add to Reader. And, Technorati is also in the business of following the way people "tag" or characterize their posts. So let's say you wanted to track all of the posts that bloggers have labeled "classroom." Just go to tinyurl.com/5fgu7r and, if you like what you see, copy and paste the address into Google Reader and look for the "Subscribe" link at the top of the results. Obviously, you can substitute any keyword you like at the end of the address above.

RSS Feeds for News Group Searches

You can also search Internet news groups and get an RSS feed of the results. Can you guess which company makes this possible? That's right. Google, as in Google Groups. Just go to Groups.Google.com, do a search, and in the results, click on the link of the group where the posting came from (i.e., bit.listserv.edtech). Again, just copy and paste the address. Beware that a search feed of newsgroups can bring back all sorts of irrelevant content, so you may want to spend some time refining your search to match your interests.

RSS Feeds for Other News Outlets

Another way to get continually updated news about various topics is to use the feeds provided by Moreover.com. It offers a huge list of predefined topic searches (tinyurl.com/2bw7c). You can find even more of these types of Moreover feeds (including ones for your favorite sports teams, the state you live in, and your favorite presidential candidate) at this page on the Syndic8.com site (tinyurl.com/yss5pb). And while most might not consider Wikipedia a "news outlet," you can also use RSS to track changes to entries that you want to follow. Just go to the "History" tab of the entry and then . . . guess what?

RSS Feeds for Bookmarks and Twitter

Feeds are also a great way to keep track of what other people are reading and Tweeting about and bookmarking for future use. But to understand those concepts, you'll have to wait until the next chapter on "The Social Web." You'll be amazed at the information you can collect.

Vanity Feeds

A good way to start building your blogging community is to find other bloggers out there who have similar interests and are writing about similar themes. One sure way to spot a blogger like that is to find one who's blogging about you! It's easy to track what other people might be saying about your blog by being alerted whenever someone is linking back to you. The easiest way to do this is to create a watchlist at Technorati for your blog address. Better yet, just search for your name (or your school's name, or town's name, and so on) at Google Blog Search and subscribe to the feed for the results. That way you can use your Reader account to find out when you or your world is a part of the "distributed" conversation that is a hallmark of the Read/Write Web.

COMBINING RSS FEEDS

Now, let's say you have a classroom full of students who each have their own Weblog. They have also set up accounts at Delicious.com (next chapter) so that they can collect relevant Web pages for the work they are doing, and they have a number of search feeds that they are tracking to collect even more information. From a teaching standpoint, if you wanted to monitor all of that information flow, it would take quite a bit of time and work. But here is a way to combine all of those collective feeds into one so that you can keep all the related work together and get a clearer picture of a student's workflow. At RSSmix.com, you just plug in as many different feeds as you like into the form, press "Create" and put the resulting feed into your aggregator, or, as we'll see in the next section, somewhere else it might be useful.

INCLUDING RSS FEEDS IN YOUR WEBLOG

Even though using Reader or some other aggregator is the easiest way to collect and view your feeds, with a little bit of work you can actually get feed results to show up on your Weblog or other Web page. Some Weblog packages have built-in ways to do this, and the instructions vary. But I'm going to show you one way to create a piece of Java script that you can then take and drop into your page wherever you want to put it.

Rss-to-javascript.com has an easy process where you just paste in the RSS feed address you want to use, choose some options to configure the result, and then click the "Generate the Javascript" button at the bottom. Copy the snippet of code that comes up and paste it into any HTML file wherever you want it to show up.

Using RSS to Create a Web Page

Even better, I think, is the ability to group together a whole bunch of different RSS feeds onto one page, and most importantly, to do that easily. Like, for example, if you were studying the crisis in Darfur in your class, and you wanted to make a constantly updated Web page of information that your students could access—a kind of "Daily Darfur" page if you will. Well, enter Pageflakes.com and Netvibes.com, two very-easy-to-use tools that allow you to do just that.

Check out the example about Darfur that I built using Pageflakes (tinyurl.com/61bup7). It combines RSS feeds on Darfur from the *New York Times* and the *Sudan Tribune,* photos about Darfur from Flickr, videos from YouTube, blog search and social bookmarking results, and more. And, even better, I can make this page collaboratively with my students. Just create an account, and then click on the yellow snowflake to start building your page. To add your own feeds, click on "Browse Flakes" from the left column, and then click the "Add RSS Feed" at the bottom of the second column from the left. Copy those feeds you want to use and paste them in one at a time. When you're done, you can click the "Make Pagecast" link and configure who can join in the process and even who can access the page. Definitely a great way to start aggregating content outside of your reader.

READING RSS FEEDS

Okay, so now you have hundreds . . . er . . . dozens . . . um . . . a few RSS feeds in your aggregator or maybe even distributed on different pages on your Web site. Now comes the hard part: checking the feeds. The real job now is to make Reader or Pageflakes (or whatever other aggregator you choose to use) a part of your daily practice. Maybe you check it right after you check your e-mail. Maybe you make it your computer's homepage for a couple of weeks. Or maybe you tape up reminders in your workspaces. However you do it, you need to build up a habit of checking to see what's new on a daily basis.

If you do stick with it, you'll begin to notice some changes in the way you go about getting your information. First, odds are you'll find yourself buying fewer newspapers and magazines. I can't tell you how much money I've saved since I started building my own "Daily Me" in my Reader account. Second, you'll find that as you get more and more used to the process, you become very good at scanning the text and finding the relevant or interesting stuff without reading every word. RSS could stand for "Reading Skill: Scanning" or "Reading Skill: Synthesizing" or—you get the idea. And this is a very important skill for our students to learn as well. As I've said, they are only going to be more and more inundated with information, and if they can learn early on to create relevant connections to the ideas and sources they need and then be efficient readers, it will serve them very well in their futures.

RSS is a powerful, flexible tool that I think will be changing our information gathering habits for years to come. If you don't try any other tool in this book, you simply have to start using RSS. Remember: Resistance is futile.

Here are some cool RSS feeds to get you started:

- Airport Delays: tinyurl.com/2snz9z
- Weather: tinyurl.com/5c4m8h
- Earthquake Notification: tinyurl.com/220pwd
- Techbargains: tinyurl.com/5q5sw4
- Word of the day: tinyurl.com/7ylnw
- Ebay: tinyurl.com/5egkve

6 The Social Web

Learning Together

Whether it's blogs or wikis or RSS, all roads now point to a Web where little is done in isolation and all things are collaborative and social in nature. As evidenced by wikis, the biggest, most sweeping change in our relationship with the Internet may not be as much the ability to publish as it is the ability to share, connect, and create with many, many others of like minds and interests. These social connections, these "Small Pieces Loosely Joined" as author David Weinberger so eloquently put it in the title of his book, are where the real power and potential of the Read/Write Web lies for educators and students. The collaborative construction of knowledge by those willing to contribute is redefining the ways we think about teaching and learning at every level.

The social Web says that we have many friends out there just waiting to be found and connected to, and those friends have other friends (friends of a friend or "FOAF") who can just as easily connect with us and point us to new and interesting information or learning. You can almost visualize this network of individual nodes of people, connected by ideas and passions, constantly shifting and changing as new connections are found and old ones are reconsidered. Finally, it also means that we're willing to share our ideas and resources with the network for its betterment, because we get back just as much if not more.

Worldwide, well over 1 billion people are now online, and the ways in which they are connecting and creating together are literally exploding. The power of social interaction, as evidenced by Wikipedia, for instance, is immense, and is being harnessed in all sorts of new and creative ways. And, once again, the implications for teaching and learning are significant as well.

Because of these tools, we can build complex networks of resources to tap into, allowing us to find more information, more teachers, and more learning.

This vision is much different from the traditional classroom in which most student work is done in isolation, never finding connection to a larger whole that might be produced by the class in its entirety. That's not to say that in this new world students don't do their own work. But it does mean that responsibility for that work is in some way shared by those interacting with it, the readers and commentators from within the classroom or outside, if allowed. Learning is a continuous conversation among many participants.

WELCOME TO THE TWITTERVERSE!

Nowhere is this continuous conversation becoming more obvious than with the explosion of Twitter, a "microblogging" tool that has grown by leaps and bounds since its introduction in 2006. While the concept of Twitter seems a bit mundane, the implementation by online educators as a powerful professional development and communications tool is anything but.

Originally, Twitter was created as a way to send quick updates to anyone who was "following" the person posting the update. (Twitter limits you to 140 characters per "tweet." See Figure 6.1.) So, for instance, if you have family members that are spread out around the world, each could be posting "tweets" about what they were doing at any given moment, and those updates would appear on the screens of all of the relatives who had asked to get them. A way to track the clan, so to speak. Seems innocuous enough, right?

What's evolved, however, is something much more interesting. Following other educators on Twitter creates a "network at my fingertips" phenomenon where people ask questions and get answers, link to great blog posts or resources, or share ideas for projects as they go through the day. For many, it's become a running river of conversation and ideas that has cemented their connections to the community and made the network even more palpable.

Just now, for instance, as I've been writing this section, I've been watching the "tweets" appear in my Nambu (the tool I use to catch my updates) window, and I've learned all sorts of things from the 150 or so people in my network that I "follow." For instance, I've been reading along as the network has been helping Dean Shareski (shareski is his Twitter name) from Moose Jaw, Saskatchewan, troubleshoot his iChat video. And author Dan Gillmor (dangillmor) just put up a tweet about Microsoft's new search engine named "Bing." Meanwhile, educator Sylvia Martinez (smartinez) in California is off to see her son graduate from college with many in the Twitterverse wishing her well.

It's that blend of the professional and the personal that makes Twitter such a cool tool on so many levels. Some people have described it as a "sixth

Figure 6.1 Twitter keeps your network at your fingertips. "Tweets" from those you follow show as updates on your homepage, and you can send your own 140-character or less "tweet" from the form at the top of the page.

sense" in terms of the network; you feel more a part of the larger conversation, more a part of the community. And, as with all good Read/Write Web networking tools, you get smarter.

If you want a sense of how Twitter changes the game, check out the great "Twitter Collaboration Stories" wiki that's hosted by Nancy White (tinyurl.com/yw7sa8). There are dozens of examples, ranging from individuals tapping into the Twitter network for recommendations to examples of Twitter's role in covering world upheavals like last year's elections in Iran, to getting on-demand tech support. It's a pretty amazing, and potentially addicting, tool once you get into it. (That addicting part is why I also follow "InnerTwitter" at Innertwitter.com. Check it out and you'll see why.)

Getting started with Twitter is not hard at all. Just go to Twitter.com and sign up for an account. The first step is to start "following" a few folks and get into the habit of reading their "tweets." To follow someone, just go to their Twitter page (for instance, mine is twitter.com/willrich45) and click the "follow" button toward the top left. Then, when you are logged in and on your personal Twitter page (Twitter.com/yourloginnamehere) you can see all of the tweets from those folks you are following as they come in. (Put a pop-up on your calendar to remind you.) Pretty quickly, you'll see some tweets with an @ sign and another name after it, as in @shareski. This is a great way to find other folks to follow because the @ sign is the way Twitterers respond to one another. Click on that new name, read their tweets, and decide whether you want to follow them as well.

Or, you can find new people to follow by using a variety of directories. Since the last edition of this book, all sorts of resource sites have sprung up for teachers who want to connect with other Twittered souls. Try, for example, the exhaustive "Directory of Learning Professionals (& Others) on Twitter" (tinyurl.com/adcdtn) or check out the fast-growing "Twitter for Teachers" wiki for connections or ideas (tinyurl.com/dmhgvh). And one last suggestion from my own practice: Make good use of Search.Twitter.com. Just yesterday I started reading Daniel Goleman's new book *Ecological Intelligence,* and when I decided to see what tweets there were out there that included that title, I was instantly connected to other people and conversations that really added to my reading and understanding of the book, and grew my network in the process.

Getting people to "follow" you is a bit more difficult. Here are three suggestions. First, enlist some friends or colleagues to join you in this venture. Nothing like having some folks you know in the face-to-face world to share your tweets with. Second, use that @ sign. If you see someone tweet a question, tweet them back by putting @ in front of their Twitter name and letting them know what you think. Even if they don't "follow" you, they will see your reply. And finally, share your own learning on Twitter. I really value those folks who are posting links or experiences that impact my own thinking and learning. The more you participate, the more followers you'll get.

The educational examples of Twitter use are growing quickly. Some schools are beginning to use it as a way to communicate with parents and others in the community. Check out Westlake High School in Austin, Texas, for instance (twitter.com/whschaps). There you can find the pretty typical daily notices, but you'll also find links to student work or live presentations, new Web tools that might be of interest, and relevant articles for parents on a variety of topics.

For students, Twitter can once again be a boon or a bane. Imagine if we could help our students use the tool to build learning-on-demand environments like the Twitter community. But while we can block people from following us, Twitter is a bit too Wild West for most school situations, although there are exceptions. (As an alternative, Edmodo.com has set up a free service for educators that does much of what Twitter does and more. It's a great way to get your students started with safe and appropriate microblogging.) The "Twitter in Academia" post at the AcademicHack blog (tinyurl.com/25u2cx) has a number of ways to start integrating Twitter into the classroom. You can use the cell phone feature of Twitter (assuming you can use cell phones in your school) to get instant feedback to a formative-assessment type question. Or as a "public notepad" for sudden inspiration.

Or, you could do like Baltimore foreign language teacher R. Richard Wojewodzki (twitter.com/teachpaperless), who uses Twitter as a way of having students collect snippets of information, keep a running assessment of what they know, and build vocabulary and grammar skills. In a great post on his blog that details the process, he says, "more and more I see Twitter as an excellent resource for assessing several of the skills that are fundamental to learning and living such as: the ability to make mistakes and immediately get positive critical feedback [and] the ability to take part in a communal discussion" (Wojewodzki, 2009).

But regardless of how you might think about Twitter in the classroom, remember, the short (140 character or less) lesson is this: Think about Twitter for yourself first. It's a great place to connect and learn with others who share your passions.

SOCIAL BOOKMARKING SERVICES

With more than 10 billion pages of information on the Web already and millions more being added each year, it's no wonder people are starting to feel overwhelmed by the Internet. Search engines like Google and Alta Vista do a good job of helping find what we might be looking for. But as we all know, sometimes their algorithms to determine what's most relevant or important don't always hit the mark. And even though we now know that RSS feeds can help us track new hits to those search terms, they suffer from the same limitations. It's starting to feel like you need your own army to help you keep track of all the information you might need or want.

Well guess what? The army has arrived. Millions of people have begun using public, online bookmarking services where they can save links, annotate them with unique keywords or "tags" to organize them, and then share them with the world. (Figure 6.2 shows some typical tags.) So, for instance, if you find a great site that lists the 50 best free software programs for teachers, in the process of saving the link to your personal account, you might attach the words "education," "software," "free stuff," or whatever else you find relevant. What these services do that's social is take all of the entries that are tagged the same way and connect them, and then connect all of the people who posted those links in the first place. So if I bookmarked a site and tagged it "free" and "software," odds are pretty good we would find each other and learn from each other's efforts. Suddenly, it's easy to find all sorts of other people who have the same interests or passions as you do. And in doing so, you're creating your own community of researchers that is gathering relevant information for you. So, social bookmarking sites complete the circle: RSS lets us read and connect with what others write; now we can read and connect with what others read as well.

Take this example from a social bookmarking site named Delicious.com that we'll talk more about later. Let's say you run across "Jane's E-Learning Pick of the Day" (Janeknight.Typepad.com), which is a great site for those looking to incorporate the newest tools into their own learning and their classrooms. You want to find out what other sites might offer similar information. When you bookmark this site at Delicious, you'll immediately be linked to everyone else who has also bookmarked the site. Now, most people added the tags "elearning" and "technology" when they saved the link. But here are some of the other tags that people have used when saving "Jane's E-Learning Pick of the Day:" "blog," "edu-blog," "pedagogy," "resources," "onlinelearning," "tool," "learning," "schools," "edtech," "guide," "reference," "read_this," "mediabase," "elearning20," and "articles" (tinyurl.com/ytvpfd). Delicious gives you the ability to click on any of those tags to be connected to other resources that might be similar to that site. The community points the way.

But there's more. In the process of creating this community, you are participating in the creation of a new way of organizing information as well.

Figure 6.2   Tags or keywords are becoming the tools that we use to organize our own pieces of the Web.

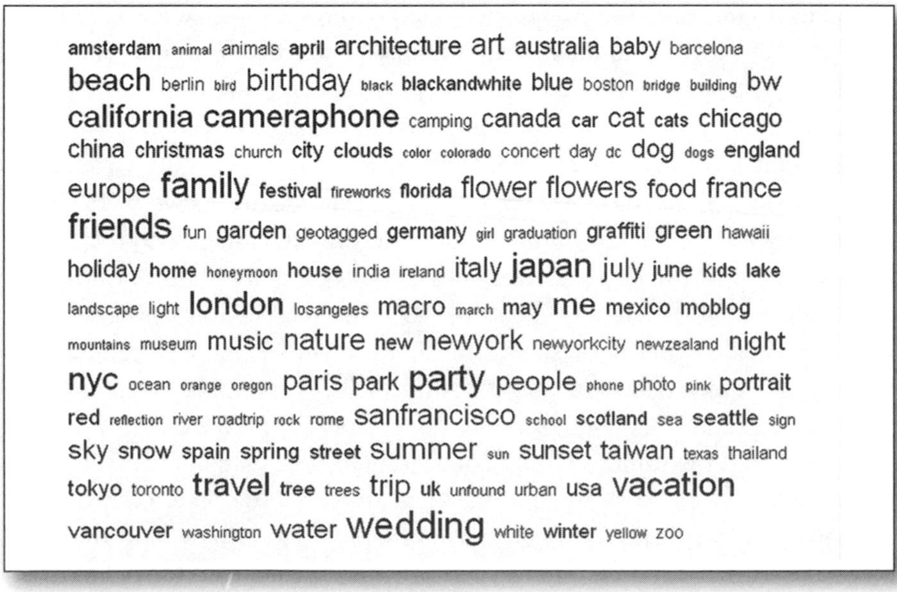

amsterdam animal animals april architecture art australia baby barcelona beach berlin bird birthday black blackandwhite blue boston bridge building bw california cameraphone camping canada car cat cats chicago china christmas church city clouds color colorado concert day dc dog dogs england europe family festival fireworks florida flower flowers food france friends fun garden geotagged germany girl graduation graffiti green hawaii holiday home honeymoon house india ireland italy japan july june kids lake landscape light london losangeles macro march may me mexico moblog mountains museum music nature new newyork newyorkcity newzealand night nyc ocean orange oregon paris park party people phone photo pink portrait red reflection river roadtrip rock rome sanfrancisco school scotland sea seattle sign sky snow spain spring street summer sun sunset taiwan texas thailand tokyo toronto travel tree trees trip uk unfound urban usa vacation vancouver washington water wedding white winter yellow zoo

This is another one of those dramatic shifts the Read/Write Web is bringing about. Back in the old days, we used to rely on librarians and others to sort and categorize information for us. These traditional taxonomies have been with us for a long time and they worked well because trained professionals using a consistent process were doing the sorting. That's why we're usually able to find what we're looking for in a library or on a subject-specific search site like Yahoo.com. But today, when we now have the power to organize vast libraries of information on our own, the process is being run by millions of amateurs with no real training in classification.

Not to worry, however, because as with many topics on the new Net, users of social bookmarking systems have created a new concept to deal with the change: the tool is no longer a taxonomy but a "folksonomy." The idea is that in working with your community of researchers, new tagging systems will emerge and become accepted that will allow us all to participate in the process. Although this might be seen as chaotic and not as effective as traditional methods, by being able to apply many tags to one particular link, we get the added potential of seeing how others might interpret or use resources that we share. Thus, we get connected to information in ways that traditional libraries cannot duplicate. And the more people contribute to the creation of folksonomies, the more valuable they become to all who participate.

And it won't end there. The idea of tagging our own content is spreading—to digital photography (as we'll see later with Flickr), to multimedia, even to documents and presentations. (And of course, to our blogs.) The more such "metadata" that we can apply to the content we create, the more easily it will be connected to other relevant artifacts, continuing the process of joining the many pieces of the Web in flexible and dynamic ways and bringing us closer to the information we need and desire.

This move toward a more socially negotiated categorization of content has interesting and, I think, powerful ramifications for teachers and students. Obviously, if we are to be expected to participate in the construction of "folksonomies" to save the information that we find, it will require us to redefine the processes we currently use in relative isolation. Our personal organizational systems for content may need revision to fit with a more communal model. And it's worth our while to do this because this more social model has the potential to lead us to more and better information. But social bookmarking also challenges us to rethink the way our students and we treat the information we find. Traditionally, we emphasize keeping track of where our research comes from. But in this new construct, it will become even more important to know how to retrieve it within the folksonomies created with our community of researchers (Educause Learning Initiative, 2005).

Now, there are many of these social bookmarking sites that have been created in the past couple of years. But two, Diigo and Delicious, have come to the forefront of the pack for some very different reasons. Once again, these are both free services that any teacher or student can access on the Web. As with other sites, although the content you'll find here is primarily safe and in good taste, take the time to become familiar with both before you use them in the classroom.

Let's start with Diigo, which continues to be one of my favorite tools on the Read/Write Web. Diigo is a tool that not only allows you to begin constructing your own little piece of the Web, it's a way of organizing it for yourself and for those you are collaborating with. I use it to store sites that deal not just with education and technology, but also for sites related to journalism, parenting, environment, kids, and the "state of the world." Whenever I find something that interests me, I add it to my archive of sites. I have thousands of sites saved, and I find myself coming back regularly to retrieve ideas or quotes.

But Diigo also has some unique features that extend our ability to read and write socially in compelling ways. Not only can we bookmark the pages we find interesting, we can actually annotate and highlight them for ourselves or with others. More on that in a minute.

As with most of these tools, setting up a Diigo account is easy. Just go to the site and click on the "Create New Account" link. Pick a unique username, and because you might want to share this with your students at some point, pick something they might remember. You'll get an e-mail validation to confirm your registration. Once you've set up your account, you'll want to add the "Diigolet" link to your browser toolbar. Just click on the Diigolet link in the left-hand column once you've logged in and then drag the icon to your toolbar. Whenever you land on a Webpage that you want to save, just click on the Diigolet button and you'll see all sorts of options to work with.

For argument's sake, let's say you land on the overview of connectivism by George Seimens at tinyurl.com/cx8n3. (Good reading, by the way.) First, you can simply save the site by clicking on the "Bookmark/Share" button once you've opened up your Diigolet toolbar. When you do, a form pops up that has the URL and title already filled in and also gives you some options in terms of adding some "meta" information to the page (see Figure 6.3). You can add tags to the page, as I mentioned before, and in this case, we might use words like "learning," "education," and "connectivism." Remember that every subsequent page that you bookmark with one of those same tags will now be collected with all the others. Your personal folksonomy is under construction.

You can choose to keep your bookmark private, or you can let other Web surfers know that you saved it as well. In fact, if you want to start connecting to other people who share your interests, Diigo will point you to other folks who have publicly saved the site. (Personally, 99 percent of what I bookmark is public for that reason.) In addition, you can add some comments

Figure 6.3 Using the Diigolet toolbar allows you to quickly bookmark interesting or relevant resources on the Web and share them with the world.

or notes to help you remember what it was that you found interesting or important about the page.

Finally, you can share your bookmark to a specific group of people that you either invite personally or that sign up to share in your interest. In the form, just click on "Share to Groups" and then select "Create a Group." As you go through the process of setting up a group, you can either make it private or public. If you make it private, you can then invite other Diigo users who you know to join that group, and only they will share in the bookmarks you save.

But the best part about Diigo is that you can use it collaboratively not just to save pages but to annotate important sections and even leave notes on the page for selected others to see (see Figure 6.4). On the Diigolet toolbar, you'll see the ability to "Highlight" and add "Sticky Notes." If you want to see a compelling example of how it works, open up this article, "Is

Technology Producing a Decline in Critical Thinking and Analysis?" at tinyurl.com/cq5pck once you've activated your Diigo account. From the comments from the ten or so people who have annotated the page, you get the idea pretty quickly that it's not technology that's causing a decline in critical thinking, it's our lack of understanding of how to use technology well.

Highlighting or annotating is really easy. Just select the piece of text you want to comment on and then click "highlight" in the toolbar. If you want to add a "sticky note," just mouse over the highlighted selection and select "Add Sticky Note." From there, you'll have other options to work with. Whenever you return to that page, all of your notes and the public notes of others will be there for you to reread or add to. It's very cool.

There is one last feature that sets Diigo apart, and that is that when you bookmark a page with your Diigolet tools, you're not just capturing a link;

Figure 6.4 By combining the thoughtful use of tags with RSS, you can use Diigo to save links that specific people or groups can receive in their RSS readers.

you are making a copy of the whole page for use later on. So, if for some reason George takes his Connectivism page down, you'll still have a copy of it in your Diigo archive. Just click on the "My Bookmarks" link from the "More" dropdown on your Diigolet toolbar and it will send you right to your archive where you can search by tag, title, or any specific word that might be in the notes. Obviously, some question the legality of saving pages from a copyright standpoint. But even though the links and public notes you save become accessible to others, only you can access the saved page from your archive. Basically, you are saving a copy just for yourself.

From a classroom standpoint, the uses of Diigo can be extremely powerful. And one of the best examples I know of is how humanities teacher Clay Burrell uses it with his student bloggers. Clay, who teaches at the Seoul American School and who blogs very provocatively at "Beyond School" (www.beyond-school.org), uses Diigo to leave feedback on his student blog posts, and has students do the same. As he puts it:

> My students have joined the Group. Now when they go to their weblogs, after logging in to their Diigo account and setting "Show Annotations > Show Group Annotations" on their Diigo toolbar, they will see the highlights of specific passages from their writing that I have left . . . and my annotations will pop up on their screen when they hover their mouse over the highlights. (Burrell, 2007)

Not only that, but the Diigo annotations page collects all of the feedback that's been left on student work from across the individual blog posts, allowing them to get a useful view over time of how their writing is evolving.

But, of course, there is much more. The fact that Diigo is Web based means that you can save from any computer and retrieve from any computer that has Internet access. I find this to be extremely convenient. (As you can tell, I'm a big fan of Web-based applications.)

You can also search the entire Diigo community for keyword matches, which is the first of many social features of the site. Obviously, once you find a result that looks interesting, you can click through to see the saved page, see the live Web site, or see a list of other people who have also saved it. Click on any of their names and you'll be taken to a page that lists the latest links that have been saved by that person. The idea, obviously, is to find other Diigo users who are finding and linking to sites that you find relevant and interesting. It's like someone else doing research for you.

Now this is where the fun starts. Diigo gives you all sorts of ways to track what other people are reading and saving. Here's one way it might work. Say you're teaching *Romeo and Juliet,* and you come across a great resource site for the book. When you save it to Diigo, you see that a dozen other people have also saved the site. When you click on one of the user names, you find that person has a whole tag dedicated to *Romeo and Juliet* resources. Great! But guess what? Now that you know all about RSS, it should come as no surprise that you can subscribe to that person's *Romeo and Juliet* tag. Just click on the little RSS icon at the top of the search box, take the address of the page that comes up and go add it to your Reader account. Then, any time that person saves a site about *Romeo and Juliet,* you'll be notified. In addition, you can "subscribe" to people and get all of their bookmarks, or you can subscribe to individual tags and get anything anyone in the Diigo universe saves with that tag. This is where the true power of social software combined with RSS lies.

Okay, now let's think about this some more. What if you set up a Diigo account for your class of students? (I'm going to assume all of your students have Google Reader accounts by this point.) First, you could have your students subscribe to the feed of a particular tag you created just for that subject. That way, any time you link and comment on a site that you've found relevant to their study, they'll automatically get it too. Even better, you could create separate tags in your Diigo account with each student's name and have that student subscribe to the RSS feed for it. That way, every time you run across something you think Meredith might be interested in reading, you simply add the tag "Meredith" to it and her feed will automatically update. Think about how you could put the comments feature to good use in this example. You could insert individualized questions or other links or suggestions for follow up. In this way, you can start to use Diigo as a powerful tool for individualized instruction.

Or, if you feel comfortable, create an account in which all share the login and password and let them start saving links relevant to whatever you are studying into a class archive. As a part of the process, start building your own socially negotiated folksonomies in terms of keywords. In fact, you could ask them to add their first names as keywords and in that way be able to track who is adding what. Or, if you want to make sure you know who is doing what, have all of your students start their own Diigo accounts. Create a unique keyword that they can add to each site that they save, like "RJ101" for that *Romeo and Juliet* example. Then you can go into Diigo, search the community archive for "RJ101," and subscribe to the RSS feed for the results. That way anytime one of your students saves a site, you'll not only be notified, you'll know who saved it.

Individual student Diigo accounts are a no-brainer for their own research projects as well. Not only can they save and archive their sources, they can pull out relevant quotes right into the form, and they can organize the information by topic or subtopic using tags.

Diigo is also a great tool for sharing information with colleagues. If you are in a school in which four, five, or even eight people are teaching political science, either set up a Diigo group that you can share in terms of adding resources or, at the very least, create tags in your individual accounts that you can each subscribe to. It's a great way to develop a highly personalized, organized, searchable archive of information for your curriculum. Better yet, if all of your students have their own Weblogs, how hard would it be to set up a "Best Practices" tag in which you save exemplary work to share with parents, administrators, or counselors?

And, let's not understate the importance of Diigo as a professional development tool. Just getting in the habit of saving interesting or useful links can be a huge asset in and of itself. And remember that Diigo allows you to mark individual links or whole folders as private, so you can use the same account for personal reasons as well.

You can also add Diigo feeds to a particular Web page. Many schools use it to automatically excerpt relevant and interesting stories about education right to a parents' page on the school Web site. (Refer to the RSS chapter for details on how to do this.) It's just one more way of finding and sharing information with a minimum of effort.

On the other hand, Delicious approaches the social bookmarking concept a bit differently (see Figure 6.5). Whereas Diigo is about saving content, Delicious is all about sharing links in as easy a way as possible. But although it may not have all of the flexibility and power that Diigo has in terms of search, annotation, and archiving, its simplicity makes it an equally powerful tool for teachers and students. And to be honest, from a personal learning standpoint, I like Delicious even better.

To Delicious, the tag is everything. Literally. One look at the "save dialogue" box tells you that aside from the site address, the most important piece of information is the label or tag you give it. Yes, you can add some annotation to the link, but finding and connecting to relevant information is not done through search; it's done through the tag. Any description you add to your link will be just for your own use. If you want to find what anyone else has saved using the same tag, just put the tag word at the end of the following address: Delicious/tag/yourtaghere.

Like Diigo, the folks at Delicious are kind enough to provide RSS feeds for all of their tags. And the feed address is almost too simple. If I want to follow what people are saving about education, for example, the URL for my Google Reader account is Delicious/rss/tag/education. Just replace the last word with whatever term you want to follow and you have your feed address. So really, you could do this without ever visiting the site. (By the way, most often, tags that are more than one word usually use an underline to separate the words. So, classroom Weblogs would be tagged as classroom_weblogs.)

Like Diigo, you can make this work to your advantage by creating unique tags that you share with your class or colleagues. And you could create a unique tag for each student in your class that they in turn could subscribe to

Figure 6.5   Delicious bookmarks are available for anyone to follow either by visiting the user pages or by RSS.

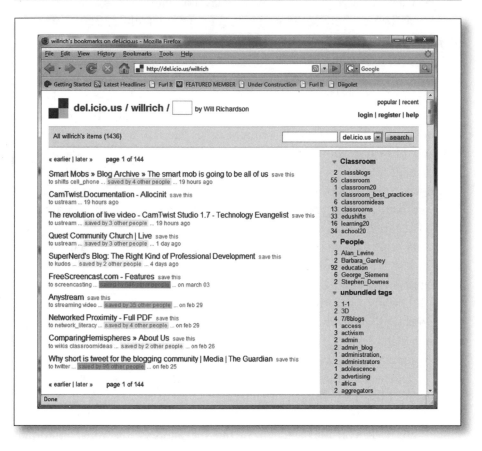

so the links you save for them would end up in their personal aggregators. Remember, however, that there is no way to prevent others outside the class from using the same tags when saving their own links. (If you make it unique enough, however, the chances will be minimized.)

Delicious is so Google-esque in its minimalist design that it doesn't even require an e-mail address to register. Just put in a username, add (or make up) your real name, create a password, and you are good to go. This makes it extremely easy to use with students, if, of course, you trust them to behave appropriately. On the other hand, it also makes it easy for you to set up student accounts, subscribe to the individual feeds, and then give them the information they need to login. This way, they are responsible for whatever content appears in their links list. And, of course, Delicious also has a click and drag "quick save" button that you can add to your browser toolbar. You'll see it when you go through the sign-up process.

Just like with Diigo, teachers who use Delicious successfully think a lot about the tagging folksonomy they set up. You could have students all tag their links with RJ101 as in the example above—any tag will work for collaborative class efforts as long as it's unique. Here's an example from a community college chemistry class: tinyurl.com/6pr69r.

Now, not to overwhelm you, but sites like Diigo and Delicious have spawned all sorts of add-on tools to make your process even more interesting, flexible, and hopefully enjoyable (tinyurl.com/cfjhpk).

A couple more twists on this social bookmarking story. If you want to start connecting socially around the books you read, try LibraryThing.com or Shelfari.com. Just start a free account that allows you to create an online catalog of all of the books in your physical library, and then you can add notes, descriptions, and, of course, tags that describe what they are about. The best part is, however, that you and your students can then connect with everyone else in the community who has also cataloged and tagged that book. It's a great way to expand your discussion of literature and to get ideas for further reading.

But regardless of how you do it, the idea that we can now use social networks to tap into the work of others to support our own learning is an important concept to understand. It's another example of how the collective contributions created by the Read/Write Web are changing the way we work and learn.

7 Fun With Flickr

Creating, Publishing, and Using Images Online

The easiest place for teachers and students to begin experimenting with creating and publishing content other than text is with digital photography, a technology that is becoming more and more accessible every day. Fairly high-resolution digital cameras can be had for as little as $100 these days, and most are easy enough for even elementary school students to use productively. And some camera phones can shoot pictures that are of a high-enough quality to be used in the classroom. And simple software to edit and resize these photos is available for free on the Web. In short, teachers and students can now include digital images in their list of things they can create in the classroom.

More importantly, in the context of the Read/Write Web, there are a growing number of ways to publish these photos to the Web easily and cheaply. In fact, some of the best photo-hosting sites offer free hosting for quite a large number of photos, and they allow users to create albums and multimedia shows that can be shared with friends and family.

But it doesn't end there, and from an educational standpoint, this is where the real fun starts. Imagine not only being able to put your own or your students' photos on the Web to share with other audiences—what if you could invite other people from around the globe to have discussions about those images? What if you and your students could annotate them with your own descriptions and observations? What if you could become a part of a community that contributes images of similar topics for you to consume? And what if you could consume those images via an RSS feed so anytime a new picture was added about a topic you were studying it would automatically come to you?

INTRODUCING FLICKR

That's the potential of Flickr.com, which has become the Web-based digital photography portal of choice for many educators. To be sure, there are other online sites that offer to host images, but Flickr has evolved into something much more than just a photo publishing space. And, since the last edition of this book, it's evolved into a video-hosting site as well. Personally, I think Flickr is one of the best sites on the Web. It's true social software where the contributors interact and share and learn from each other in creative and interesting ways. And for that reason, it's educational potential is huge.

Why consider posting images or video to the Web in the first place? From a classroom standpoint, think about the ability to capture daily events or highlights and easily share those with parents, community, and colleagues. Field trips, speakers and visitors, special projects, and much more could become a part of any classroom's "photo stream" and could be a great way of sharing the teaching and learning experience. And what better way to celebrate the good work that students do every day than by putting it online for all (or some) to see?

Before we get into the details, however, this disclaimer: As with most other things on the Web, no one can guarantee with absolute certainty the quality or appropriateness of the content on Flickr. Flickr members self-police the 1–2 million photos and videos that are uploaded daily, and content filters keep the most troublesome photos at bay (unless, of course, the filter settings get changed). The vast majority of the photos on the site are appropriate for all, and there are some absolutely wonderful photos on just about any topic that you can find there. (Try clicking the "most interesting" link after doing a search.) That being said, however, take the time to become familiar with the potentials and risks of Flickr before you bring it into your classroom, and make time to convey your expectations and to teach appropriate use of the site to your students.

First, let's run through the basics. Flickr is free as long as you don't publish more than 100 MB of images and more than two 500 MB videos (about 90 seconds each) a month. If you develop some basic editing and file-saving skills to manage file size, this means that you could easily post 500 images a month without too much worry. Only the last 200 will be viewable in your "photostream," however. (One important note: If your free account is inactive for 90 days, it will be deleted. It's good practice in general to always keep copies of your photos offline as well.) If you do want to go beyond that, a "pro" account for $24.95 a year gives you unlimited uploads, unlimited storage, and unlimited viewing ability. (Some of my "friends" on Flickr have over 10,000 photos online!) You need to register with Flickr in order to publish photos or take part in discussions, and you need a valid e-mail address to do that. If you are thinking of using this with a class of students, you could create one login for all of them to share or have them create their own accounts. Just follow the pretty standard login procedures from Flickr's homepage.

Once you've set up your account, you're ready to get started. Adding images to your Flickr folder is easy; just click on the upload link, find the image on your computer that you want to publish, and click "Upload." If you like, you can also upload images using an e-mail function that you set up in the "Your Account" section. And, most photo and video editing software now comes with a Flickr upload link built in. You may have to dig around a bit to find it.

Just to be clear, you should do all of your photo editing and adjusting on your computer before you upload your image to Flickr. (Or, if you don't have editing capabilities on your computer, upload the picture to Picnik.com where, when you are done editing, you can automatically send it to your Flickr account. Too easy!) During the upload process, you can restrict access to what you publish by selecting from three different options. If you opt to restrict viewing access to "Friends" or "Family," for instance, only those people who you have "Invited" as members of those groups will be able to see them. This means that you can work with your students behind closed screens, so to speak, exchanging photos and having conversations that no one else can read or join. From a K–12 standpoint, it's one of the best features of Flickr. Or, of course, you can allow anyone to see and interact with an image by making it "Public."

And, as with any good social software these days, Flickr will ask you to tag your photos with keywords so that, much like with Delicious.com, you can begin to connect your photos with other people's photos, and you can build an organizational foundation for your uploaded work. The more tags you give, the better the chance that your photos will find others of the same subject.

And finally, on the question of safety and appropriateness, Flickr does allow for the creation of private groups where you and your students (and other invited guests) can work in your own space. Also, while the social aspect of Flickr allows for comments and connections to be made around photos, you can turn off discussion on any or all of the photos that you submit.

LEARNING WITH FLICKR

So what can you do with Flickr in the classroom? David Jakes, an educational technology coordinator from Illinois who blogs often about using the Web to create digital stories, has a number of great suggestions (tinyurl.com/38wsm5). Among them are to create presentations and slide shows, cobble together virtual field trips, illustrate poetry, document school work, teach about social software, and teach geography by integrating with Google Earth. (More on that in a minute.)

One of the most useful tools in Flickr is the annotation feature, which allows you to add notes to parts of the image simply by dragging a box across an area and typing text into a form. Afterward, when you drag your mouse across the picture, the boxes and annotations pop up.

For example, Sophie, a third grader at Tim Lauer's Lewis Elementary School, used the Flickr annotation tool to help identify the different features of a model she had created of Jane Goodall's camp in Africa (tinyurl.com/2tn3kl) (see Figure 7.1). So, when you drag your mouse around the photo, notes pop up that identify what you are looking at, such as Goodall's typewriter, a map Goodall used to plan her expeditions, and the pots and pans Goodall used to cook. Or, if you want another great example, look at Alan Levine's incredibly great presentation "What Can We Do With Flickr?" which is run entirely through an annotated photo on, that's right, Flickr (tinyurl.com/2kly3j).

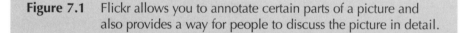

Figure 7.1   Flickr allows you to annotate certain parts of a picture and also provides a way for people to discuss the picture in detail.

In and of itself, the annotation tool offers a great deal of possibilities. Imagine being able to annotate portions of a Civil War battlefield or a fetal pig dissection for students to access and review. Or, as a test of their knowledge, ask them to annotate what they see. Remember, you and your students can use any digital image at your disposal, whether you have taken it or found it on the Web, as long as you attribute the source. (The copyright issues of using an image already found on the Web fall under the Fair Use Doctrine in this instance.) So, if you find a photo at the New York Public Library's extensive photo archive that you'd like to work with, you can move it to a private space in Flickr, add a link to the original, and make it a part of your curriculum. In addition, at this writing there are over 25 million photos posted at Flickr that carry Creative Commons copyright licenses, which allow for their legal reuse in any number of ways (tinyurl.com/26ynlo). Using Creative Commons licenses, the photographers who publish their own photos to Flickr can indicate what types of uses they will allow for those images. In most instances, these content providers simply ask for attribution and that images not be used for commercial purposes.

Another great aspect of Flickr is the ability to start online discussions about the images you post by adding comments under any particular photo. And remember, these conversations can be held in private depending on what level of security you have assigned your photos. What this means is that you can ask your students to interpret or comment further on what they see, all in the spirit of teaching them how to come to a collaboratively created understanding of a particular image's use or meaning. And, even better, you can subscribe to these discussions via the RSS feed that Flickr creates for your "Recent Comments." This way, you can track what your students are writing without having to visit the photo page.

But the real power of Flickr lies in the ways it can connect people from around the world. Each photo that gets uploaded to Flickr can have "tags" or keywords associated with it by the publisher, and those tags are then searchable. In this way, "public" images of similar themes or topics find each other, and in many cases, so do the people behind them. Some of the most popular tags, as you might guess, are "wedding," "vacation," "family," and "friends." But there's probably a photo for just about every tag you can think of. Oh, and since we're talking about RSS, don't forget that you can also "subscribe" to a particular tag so you can receive any new photos that people post with the keywords "schnauzer" or "skiing" or even "sleepwalking" if you like. Just copy the URL www.flickr.com/photos/tags/sleepwalking (using whatever tag you want at the end) and then paste it into the "Add Subscription" line in your Google Reader. (It works with Pageflakes or Netvibes, too.)

If your students are studying other countries or cultures, Flickr can be an incredible resource of images and information, and with teacher moderation, there can even be opportunities to meet and learn with other people and students from far-flung places. By leaving a comment on the photos they find, students can potentially learn more about the photographer and the photograph. And again, this can be done in a safe way without students divulging any personal information.

Even better is using Flickr with Google Maps and Google Earth to begin to give a global sense of the world in photos. Not only can you make it so that the photos you upload to Flickr open up to the place where they were taken on Google Earth, but you can begin to see all the other Flickr photos that have been taken in that same spot as well. You start by finding the exact latitude and longitude of where a picture was taken. To do that, go to Google Maps (Maps.Google.com) and enter the address or the attraction into the search line. (For instance, typing in "Mt. Rushmore" will take you to the exact spot on the South Dakota map.) Now, click on the "Link to This Page" link at the top right of the map. In the URL of the page that appears will be the latitude and longitude information you need right after the letters "11" in the address. It will look something like this:

11=43.8828,-103.459969

Now, go back to your photo in Flickr and add tags that show these coordinates. Here's the form: "geo:lat=43.8828" for the latitude tag, and "geo:lon=-103.459969" as the longitude tag. (And yes, that is a minus sign in the longitude.) Add a third tag "geotagged" and you're almost ready to go. Finally, add this comment to your photo just the way it appears, but without the beginning and end quotation marks:

"Click on <a href=http://www.roblog.com/flickrfly.php>this link</a> to see this picture in <a href=http://earth.google.com/>Google Earth!</a>"

Now, when you publish the comment, click on the link, and, assuming you have Google Earth installed, it should open up and show you exactly where the photo was taken. Pretty cool! (See an example of how this works at tinyurl.com/2dztfl.)

If you want to see what other photos in the Flickr universe have been geotagged, you can use Flickr's own map tool at Flickr.com/map. Just search for a tag, like "sailing," and see what comes up. (Hint: There are boatloads of them.) Imagine your students using this to create a photo tour of your community or city—very cool.

And remember, if you find sailors from halfway around the world, you can always contact them to see if they might have some experiences to share with your students.

Organizing photos at Flickr is easy as it allows you to create separate albums for different sets of pictures. It even has a slideshow function, so you can create a series of moving images with just a few clicks of the mouse. Both of these tools can be found by clicking the "Organize" link. So, students can create their own personalized collections of photos that they themselves have taken or found on the Web, complete with annotations and discussion with others. Flickr could also serve as a student's online portfolio with digital images of her work that are annotated with reflective descriptions and commented on by peers and mentors. Or, what about using Flickr to connect students and teachers during their summer vacations, posting pictures of their travels and talking back and forth about what they are seeing and learning? That's a pretty powerful application if you ask me.

But there's more. While Flickr is all about putting photos up on the Web, it's also a great resource to use to teach all sorts of other skills and literacies. First of all, there is some really great photography that people are publishing for public consumption and discussion. (For instance, take a look at this slide show of incredibly beautiful plants and flowers: tinyurl.com/25dkcu.)

Flickr has also proven to be a valuable tool from a current events standpoint. Many times in the recent past when major news events have occurred, photos have appeared on Flickr even before large news organization Web sites. There is no better example than when Hurricane Katrina devastated parts of the Gulf Coast; Flickr became a collection place for many of the on-the-scene photos that people were able to publish. And if that doesn't convince you, check out the thousands of photos that have been uploaded of Barack Obama since his inauguration in 2009. It has become a powerful tool for amateur journalists who use their camera phones to e-mail photos right to their Flickr pages, posting images almost as they happen. (Of course, this is something that you and your students can do as well, provided you have the right phone.) There are many ways in which teachers and students can learn about news and photojournalism in this way.

That publishing stream can work two ways as well. Not only is it easy to send pictures to Flickr, but it's also easy to send images from Flickr to your aggregator, Weblog or Web page. The most obvious implementation of this is to stream all of the photos your students publish to the class homepage. This way, they are collected in an easily accessible space. If students have their own Weblogs, they can add their own photostreams as well. Think, for instance, of a student who is studying, say, clouds. Currently, over 1 million photos are tagged "cloud" in Flickr's database, and more are being added every day. Those pictures could be brought right to the blog via the RSS feed for that tag, or via the "Blog This" feature that appears with every photo you can view on the site. Or, at the very least, they could be collected in the student's aggregator (which, by now, I'm sure he has set up!).

FLICKR IN PRACTICE

A number of educators have already started finding creative uses for Flickr in a variety of disciplines. Brian Crosby, a fourth-grade teacher in Sparks, Nevada, has used Flickr photos extensively with his students in ways that engaged their writing and also supplemented their study of science, social studies, reading, and even math (tinyurl.com/cr85k9). They have chronicled field trips, captured projects, and recorded virtual guest speakers as a part of their Flickr photo stream. (And then check out how they used many of them on their "Reno Bike Project" wiki at tinyurl.com/dbqtnd.) Using some of the Flickr add-on tools, they even made magazine covers and movie posters of some of the pictures they took.

Then there is Steve Brooks, who writes the Edugadget Weblog where you can find "plain-talking technology reviews for teachers" (www.edugadget.com). Brooks especially likes the Creative Commons section of Flickr where teachers can be sure students are using images appropriately.

"The thing I like about getting images from Flickr is the students can see that there are real people behind the images, not some generic, faceless Web site," writes Brooks on his Weblog. "Real people, like them, have created the pictures, shared them with everyone else, and usually only asked to be credited. There are all kinds of lessons to be taught in those actions" (Brooks, 2005b).

Brooks suggests all sorts of activities: for example, "photo field trips," in which students search for images from a certain part of the world from at least three different people and then put them together in a PowerPoint presentation with reflection on what they found. Or "random writes," in which students go to the main screen in the Creative Commons section, type the first word that comes to mind into the tag field, take the first image in the photostream that comes up and write a story about it. And, one of my favorites, "Make It Mine," where students take images from the Creative Commons section, modify and "remix" them on their own computers using a paint or photo-editing package, and then republish to Flickr with credit to the work's original owner.

David Jakes decided to create an imaged version of the poem "Chicago" by Carl Sandburg by linking Flickr photos to the more tag-able words in the poem. So, for instance, he took the words "railroads," "stormy," "city," "big shoulders," and others and associated Flickr photos with them. He describes this process in his blog:

> I was thinking of all the interpretive possibilities with literature and with the shear volume of photography at Flickr, the endless possibilities to create visual stories with Flickr, that could link Flickr photography with works from authors like Sandburg, or, of course,

our students. Imagine taking a piece of beautiful photography and a likewise beautiful poem and merging the two together in a twenty-first century product . . . *that would be the result of twenty-first century open-source thinking and learning.* (Jakes, 2005)

MORE FLICKR FUN

People love Flickr so much that there have been a host of creative applications built around it, some of which also have interesting uses in the classroom. "Flickr Toolbox: 100+ Tools for Flickr Addicts" " (tinyurl.com/24y5m4) has, without question, the most comprehensive list on the Web and is a great place to start. One of my favorites is Flickr Magazine Cover (tinyurl.com/2vz17j), where you can turn any one of your pictures into front-page news.

Or, how about the Flickr Color Picker, which will allow you to use a slider to adjust lightness and darkness to show you photos with that main color? Or the FlickrReplacr Bookmarklet (tinyurl.com/8ufgf), which will allow you to highlight a word on any Web page and swap in a Flickr photo with that tag? Or "FlickrStorm" (tinyurl.com/ogzva), which is a tool that allows you to compile sets of photos based on the tags they were uploaded with (great for digital storytelling!). Or you can play "Flicktion" by having students pick a random photo from Flickr and write a story about it. Check out the stories already on Flickr at tinyurl.com/6e84jh. Or, if you want running updates of the best in Flickrphenalia, just subscribe to Alan Levine's "Flickr" tag in Delicious (tinyurl.com/rbs3pe). There's a lot out there to play with and learn.

Finally, I just want to point out a couple of ways that you can add images that you capture from your computer to Flickr. For instance, let's say that you (or your students) are doing a presentation, and you've found some great Creative Commons licensed photos on Flickr that allow you to add text, meaning you are allowed to create derivatives. (If you want to see a great set of slides like this, check out the "Digital Bites" set from Will Lion at tinyurl.com/cbse9a.) You could download the photo, bring it into PowerPoint or Photoshop, and add the words to it. But an easier (and more fun) method is to use a screen-capturing program like Skitch (at Skitch.com for Macs) or Jing (at Jingproject.com for both Windows and Macs). Jing is also a screen-casting software that I'll talk about in Chapter 8.

Both of these programs are free downloads and they allow you to capture portions of your screen and then mark up those captures with words, or in Skitch's case, highlights, arrows and other fun stuff. So, for instance, if you want students to be able to add a haiku they've written to a compelling image, bring up the image on screen, snip it into Skitch or Jing by simply dragging your mouse around the area you want, type in the poem right on the captured image, and then send directly to Flickr. Then, when it's online, make sure the student attributes the picture by adding a link to the original in a comment. Finally, put all of those poems into a set, and you have an easily created online presentation that's also easy to share.

And from a video standpoint, I'd be remiss not to mention one of my favorite combinations: Flickr and Flip. Flip video cameras (Theflip.com) are palm-sized, fairly inexpensive, high-quality movie-making machines that make the whole process about as easy as it gets. The Flip has a built-in USB connector that allows for exceedingly easy downloads from the camera to the computer, allows you to edit on the fly, and then makes uploading seamless to Flickr or YouTube. Remember, you are limited to around 90 seconds of video when using Flickr, but in many cases, 90 seconds is more than enough to make a compelling statement about the world and share it with others.

The possibilities here are pretty endless, limited only by your imagination and your own understanding of these tools. But this is the power of the Read/Write Web, being able to create and connect content through publishing in ways we never thought possible. Flickr is a great tool for introducing students not only to digital images and publishing, but also to the social conversations and collaborative learning opportunities that the Web now offers.

8 Podcasting, Video and Screencasting, and Live Streaming

Multimedia Publishing for the Masses

If there is one thing for certain it's that the explosion in the last few years of multimedia publishing on the Web is going to continue, and that more and more of what we consume online is going to be self-produced, home-made entertainment. The incredible growth of YouTube.com, Google Video, and other audio and video sites online is rattling the very foundations of television and radio, and it's no doubt going to be very interesting to see how all of it plays out in the next few years. Today we have podcasters creating their own Internet radio, videobloggers producing their own Web television, and screencasters who are capturing what happens on a computer screen, adding a bit of audio narrative, and publishing it as multimedia Web tours or stories. And, more recently, we have students and teachers who are broadcasting live to large and global audiences using live streaming tools. What's next?

This expansion of the Web into multimedia has come about quickly and is fast evolving, due primarily to the sudden explosion of broadband connectivity and cheap memory on computers. These days, it doesn't take hours to download a feature-length film, a fact that Netflix and Blockbuster are capitalizing on.

Similarly, it doesn't take an expensive computer to be able to store and play those files, as hard-drive disk space and RAM have become incredibly cheap compared to what they were just a few years ago. Those two advances have created another change in the way we consume multimedia. Whereas our computers used to play the media file as it streamed through the connection, now it simply downloads it and plays it once completely saved. It's made viewing these types of files more efficient and enjoyable, and it has pushed streaming of content further into the realm of live performance.

But whatever the technology, the simple fact is that it has become much easier to create and consume multimedia as well as text and digital images. The almost ubiquitous presence of photo-video-audio upload-it-as-you-go cell phones, and free, as-much-space-as-you-want hosting online have begun to blur many of the cultural definitions of privacy and communication that we've lived under for generations. And the upshot is that all of it has created even more in terms of the potential uses of this new Read/Write Web that we are dealing with.

PODCASTING

One of the first podcasts I ever remember listening to was by Matthew Bischoff, a teenager who had a real passion for technology and a real understanding of audience. It was obvious from the first few seconds of his regular Internet radio show that he was a young man who was not speaking to just his friends or family. He was speaking to the unknown thousands of people who started downloading and listening to Matthew's shows in late 2004 when podcasting was born. "This *is* Escape From the World" he would half-shout into the microphone, "and I'm your host Matthew Bischoff, a 13-year-old from New Jersey, podcasting from his bedroom." It was great stuff (Bischoff, 2005).

Matthew was one of the first of what has turned into tens of thousands of people who have taken the easy-publishing meme of the Read/Write Web into the world of Web radio. Podcasting is the creation and distribution of amateur radio, plain and simple. And it's the distribution piece of this that's important, because although we've been able to do digital audio for some time now, getting a lot of people to listen to it hasn't been very easy. Now it is. Many podcasts are presented by normal, everyday people just talking about things that interest them—with a bit of music mixed in. Others are more serious and focused in content, offering up the latest interesting news on a particular topic, interviews with interesting people, or recordings of interesting keynotes and presentations. And these days, most news programs, like *Meet the Press* and *60 Minutes,* and many radio shows like *Fresh Air* from NPR are also offered up as podcasts so you can take them with you and listen to them whenever you like.

In just a few short years, podcasting has become all the rage, and one of the reasons is that the barrier to entry is pretty low. Like the other technologies that I've talked about in this book, you do not need a lot of technical expertise to make it work.

Here's what you need to create a basic podcast: a digital audio recorder that can create an MP3 file, some space on a server to host the file, a blog, and something to say. That's it. That's part of why the number of new podcasts out there continues to explode. The other part of the quick success of podcasting comes from the fact that not only are they easy to create, they are easy to consume as well. And that's because of RSS.

Just like it allows people to subscribe to your Weblog, RSS allows people to subscribe to your podcast. And just like new blog content shows up in your aggregator whenever it's posted, new podcasts show up in your MP3 player whenever they are created. Say, for instance, you are subscribed to Ben Grey's "The Ed Revolution" podcast (Theedrevolution .com). Whenever you program it to do so, the free podcast aggregator software that sits on your computer will go out and check to see if Ben has a new show for you to listen to and, if so, will download it to your computer. Even better, if your MP3 player is connected to your computer at the time, the software will send it over automatically. So, conceivably, you could wake up every morning, disconnect your player from the computer and go out for that early morning run or drive with a whole list of new content to listen to.

Apple loves this, of course, because it's suddenly made the iPod (or iPhone) into a mobile radio station that can hold personalized, time-shifted content for your consumption whenever you feel like. And they also love it because of the name, even though none of this requires an iPod. It could just as easily be "audiocasting" or "blogcasting" or something else, but podcasting has stuck.

So who is podcasting? Mostly, it's people from all different walks of life with all sorts of interests. Politicians are definitely in the podcasting groove, as every candidate for the presidency in 2008 started pumping them out well before the primaries. Rightly so, they see the genre as way of getting out their respective messages. Businesses, churches, governments, and, you guessed it, schools are getting into the act as well.

The best place to start your podcasting indoctrination is to take some time to listen to a few shows. But be prepared: This is not the highly polished, professional radio you might be used to. Cracks and pops, obscure music, and "ums" and "ahs" are all a part of the podcast genre. Remember, most podcasters are just average Jills and Joes, with day jobs and kids and responsibilities, and ideas that they want to share. Try not to let production value overwhelm what might be really interesting content.

It's no surprise that Apple has incorporated support for listening and subscribing to podcasts into iTunes, its software for managing music on the iPod (see Figure 8.1). In case you're not using an iPod (and there are a lot of great alternatives out there), iTunes is free for download from the Apple site (www.apple.com/itunes/). Once you have it up and running, just go to the iTunes store homepage and click on the podcasts link in the top left section. Under the categories that come up, select "Education," and in the "More Education" box, click on K–12. There you'll see all of the top podcasts of the day as well as links to those that are featured. Click on any of the icons and you'll come to a list of the most recent episodes, which you can preview through your computer if you like. If you find it worthwhile, just click the "Subscribe" button to add it to your iTunes list. The next time you fire up iTunes, it will automatically go and check for any new episodes, download them to your computer, and synch them with your iPod when you plug it in. (For more on the complete uses of iTunes, see tinyurl.com/3y3zub.) If you find some other podcasts out there on the Web that aren't listed in iTunes, you'll need to subscribe to them manually. Just find the address of the RSS feed for the show and paste it into iTunes under the "Advanced=Subscribe to Podcast" function in the menu bar.

Figure 8.1 iTunes is Apple's free software to help you find podcasts to listen to and to list the shows you create.

Once you have some subscriptions set up, you need one more step to get your podcasts loaded directly to your MP3 player. If you leave your iPod docked and plugged into the computer at night, JuiceReceiver (tinyurl.com/fuzyg) and iTunes will do everything you need to make any new podcasts available for listening in the morning. If you don't have an iPod, you might need to use Windows Media Player to move your files around. Open Media Player and click on "Tools" then "Options," and then select the "Library" tab. From there, click the "Monitor Folders" button and "Add" the folder where JuiceReceiver stores the podcasts you are subscribed to, usually C:\Documents and Settings\your username\Application Data\iPodder\down loads (for a more detailed description of how to do this, see Jake Luddington's post on "Podcasting with Windows Media Player," at tinyurl.com/q8xksq). Then, plug in your MP3 player and use the "Sync" tab to drag and drop the files you want.

PODCASTS AND SCHOOLS

As with most of these other technologies, it's not hard to see why podcasts are making inroads in schools. One way to get into the flow of education-related podcasting is to visit the Education Podcast Network (tinyurl.com/66grdx), which lists nearly 1,000 different education-related shows. Not only is there a growing directory of educators who are doing personal podcasts, there are links to suggested classroom uses broken down both by grade level and subject.

And remember, the underlying technology here is digital recording and the idea that it is now *very easy* to create and publish these recordings. You and your students may not have iPods or MP3 players, and the good news is you don't need them to start using audio in this way. As long as you have a way to make the recording, and as long as your students have access to the Internet, you can make this work. More about that in a minute.

In general, radio broadcasting is now a reality for the vast majority of schools that can't afford radio stations. About $100 and an Internet connection is all you need to start doing regular radio shows with your students. And once again, the motivating factor, to me at least, is that the content of these shows does not have to be limited to a school or community audience. Podcasting is yet another way for them to be creating and contributing ideas to a larger conversation, and it's a way of archiving that contribution for future audiences to use.

One of my favorite examples is Radio Willow Web from the Willowdale Elementary School in Omaha, Nebraska (tinyurl.com/2z2ujz). As the Web site says, these Willowcasts are "online radio shows for kids by kids" (site shown in Figure 8.2). Each show has its own host, theme, and unique segments, which can include things such as "Bad Joke, Good Joke," "Holiday Spotlight," "Poetry Corner," and much more. It's a great example of what you can do with podcasts.

Figure 8.2   Students at Willowdale Elementary in Nebraska are podcasting about their school on a regular basis.

And then there are "Coleycasts" by the students of Brent Coley in Murrieta, California. They produced 18 "enhanced" podcasts with audio and accompanying slides on everything from the solar system to Spanish explorers during the 2008–09 school year (tinyurl.com/oj6f39). These are some great examples of kids making their learning transparent for others. Or how about "Students Teaching Students," which is a regular podcast that fifth graders at the International School of Thailand in Bangkok produce around the idea of "helping other students learn and use quality strategies for reading." On the class Gcast page (another hosting service for podcasts) you can find dozens of recordings specific to Reader's Workshop topics that third graders at the school (and others) are using to think about how to better understand the reading process and the themes, plots, and characters for the books they are reading (tinyurl.com/lgd3cr). Real work for real audiences.

But podcasting doesn't just have to be edu-radio. There are many other ways that teachers can bring the genre into the classroom. World language teachers could record and publish daily practice lessons that students could listen to at home or, if they are fortunate enough, could download to their own MP3 players. Like the Madrid Young Learners Podcasts site (tinyurl.com/5qbqze), where an English speaker tells a story via a podcast and non-English speaking listeners answer questions in English via comments. How hard would it be to make your own site like this (now that you know how to blog), with teachers enlisting native speakers from around the world to tell stories that their own students respond to?

Social studies teachers could have their students do oral histories, interviews, or reenactments of historical events. Science teachers could have students narrate labs or dissections or experiments to record their processes. Music teachers could record weekly recitals or special events as podcasts. All teachers could record important parts of what they do in the classroom that can then be archived to the class Weblog and used by students who may have missed the class or just want a refresher on what happened.

Steve Brooks over at EduGadget.com has some suggestions that schools and districts might want to think about, including guided "pod tours" of the campus on back-to-school night (perhaps created by students), or tours of art displays narrated by the artists. You could record assemblies, do new teacher orientations, have supervisors record descriptions of their departments, and record board meetings for students, teachers, and parents who are unable to attend. Principals could record weekly or monthly messages to the community, teachers, or even students. As with blogs, the possibilities are only limited by your imagination (Brooks, 2005a).

Remember, all of these ideas can be put into practice simply by recording digital audio, but the key to turning your or your students' recordings into podcasts is to publish them. That's what the Read/Write Web is all about: being able to share what you create with others. As I've said before, keep thinking about ways to add these student contributions to the larger database of learning that's out there.

GETTING STARTED WITH PODCASTING

Before you get your students podcasting, I would urge you to try it out first. Again, I think you need to experience what you are asking your students to do—not only so you can support their technical use, but also so you understand what Web publishing really feels like. Although the following may seem a bit high end, technically, podcasting is one of those technologies that can be as simple or as complex as you want it to be. And like all of these technologies, once you've done it a couple of times, it should come pretty easily.

First, you need a way to record digital audio. If you don't have a computer that has a microphone built into the monitor (like most laptops these days) you can do this by plugging a microphone into your computer to record, or by recording directly onto some MP3 players. (Some handheld devices and mobile phones also make this possible.) For instance, iPods have microphone attachments that allow you to record directly to your iPod in MP3 format (the Griffin iTalk, for one). If you have a second generation iTouch, you can use the QuickVoice Recorder app from the iTunes app store (which also works on an iPhone if you have one of those). These are great for doing mobile recordings, like on field trips or while driving (not recommended). Take some time to experiment, record, and listen to see what kind of quality you can get and whether or not it suits your needs. And you'll also need to learn how to get the recordings off of your player and onto your computer. Depending on what type of portable recorder you use, you can use iTunes or Windows Media Player to do this when you attach your player.

Making MP3 recordings on your computer is pretty easy and inexpensive as well, and generally the quality is better. In addition, you save the step of having to transfer your recording over from your handheld device. You'll need some software to capture what you record in MP3 format, and I would recommend the open-source program Audacity (tinyurl.com/4gx3j), which is free, easy to use, and is a good audio-editing program as well. (You'll also need to download Audacity's MP3 encoder at tinyurl.com/bka3e separately to translate your files into MP3s.) Remember that if you use Audacity, you need to choose "Export as MP3" under the file menu when you've finished recording and editing. And remember, too, that you can use Audacity to clean up the recordings you create on your MP3 players (see Figure 8.3 for an image of Audacity).

Figure 8.3 Audacity is a free, open-source program that makes it easy to edit and mix your audio files.

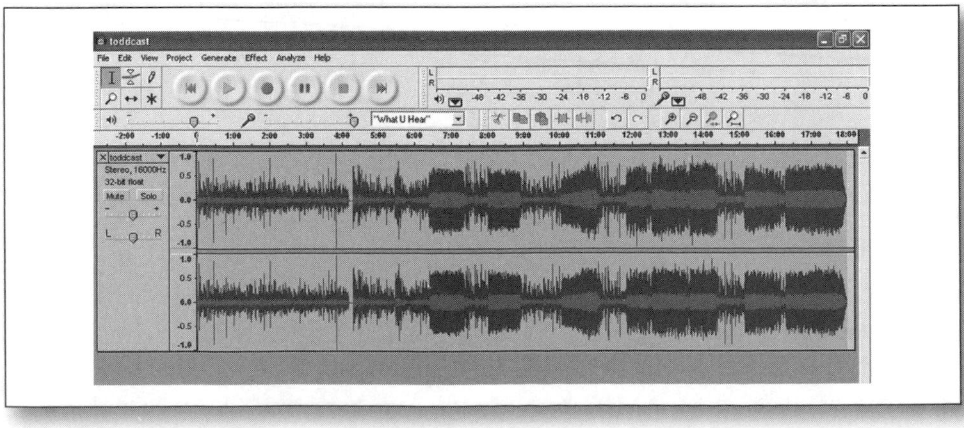

SOURCE: Used with permission of Audacity.

One other way to capture audio content for podcast is to use the free Internet telephone service Skype (Skype.com) to record interviews with people from around the world. (They can either have a Skype account as well, or they can use their regular telephones.) In fact, you can hold and record conference calls of up to five people. There are lots of recording programs out there, but I would suggest Call Recorder for a Mac ($14.95 at this writing at tinyurl.com/euc2f) and Skype Call Recorder (free at tinyurl.com/d3zlpy) for a Windows machine. And a headset microphone would really improve the quality. Just download the software, set up your Skype account, get the Skype names of the other people you want to talk to (I'm willrich45), record the phone call, and use Audacity to export it as an MP3. Personally, I think there is a huge potential for using Skype in this way in the classroom.

Once you have your "studio" ready, you need to figure out what you want to do or say for your test run. Maybe you can begin by creating short responses to things you read in the news or in the blogosphere. Or perhaps you want to create an audio tour of your classroom, interview some other teachers, recite poetry, or even sing a little bit (in my case, a very little bit). Whatever you decide to do, think about your audience, because you'll be asking your students to do the same. (You may even want to write out your first few podcasts beforehand, but I would urge you to try not to read from a prepared script.)

If you're using Audacity to record onto your computer, just plug your microphone in and click on the "Record" button. Don't worry too much about fooling around with the levels and the settings to start. Just make some short recordings and play them back to see how they sound. If you have a microphone attachment and are using your MP3 player as a recorder, you'll need to go through the synching-up process for whatever player you have to get the recorded files onto your hard drive.

When you've finished the talking part of your podcast, you might want to do a little editing and production. Using Audacity, you can easily edit out all of the "ums" and "ahs," unless of course you find they add charm to your show. (Not to jump ahead, but there is a great video/audio screencast by Matt Pasiewicz on using Audacity at tinyurl.com/bjrmo.) Even better, you can use Audacity to add intro or transition music to your work (see Figure 8.3). If you have the means to create your own digital music—GarageBand for instance—you don't have to worry about the copyright issues of using other people's work. If you can't make your own, you might surf on over to CCMixter.org to find some free-use music that's legal to add.

Here's how: After you have saved the music files to your computer, use the "Import Audio" feature under the Project section in Audacity to start editing and mixing. Start with your own recording. Press the play button to start listening, and then use the "Selection Tool" (the icon that looks like an *I* in the upper left-hand corner) to drag over the parts of the file that you want to edit out, and hit delete. When you've finished with that, import your music track the same way and then line up the timing between the tracks by using the "Time Shift Tool" (the one that looks like a two-headed arrow). You can fade one track in by using the Selection Tool and then choosing "Fade In" from the Effects section. It may look daunting, but if you play just a little, you should be able to do some editing and production in no time. Or not: Remember, one of the charms of podcasting is its unfinished quality. So don't get worn down by production if it doesn't suit you. When you're done, just "Export as MP" from the File section, and you're ready to publish.

The first step to sharing your podcast is to transfer the MP3 file you made from your computer to a server that's on the Internet. If you have a Web server at your school, that's probably your best bet. (In this case, maybe your first podcast should be one that highlights the fine work of your school's Webmaster.) But even if you don't, or even if you for some reason can't use that server, there are alternatives. The first is archive.org, which "provides free storage and free bandwidth for your videos, audio files, photos, text or software. Forever. No catches." Just sign up for a free account and upload your MP3 using their easy process. Wherever you put it, you use the unique URL that is assigned to the file to create a direct link to it in your blog or Web site. When people click the link, they'll hear your creation.

The other way to get your file on the Internet is through the blog software that you use. Most popular blog software such as WordPress now have automatic support for "enclosures" like MP3s (or any other type of file for that matter). When you create the post that describes your podcast, you'll be able to add the MP3 file to the post automatically by attaching it. (This process varies depending on your software—search for "enclosures" in the "Help" section.) This step gets the file onto a server and automatically links it in your post. And, in this case, it means that people (students) who want to listen to the audiocasts you've created can do so by simply subscribing to the RSS feed of your blog. With Blogger, this is a bit more complicated, but there is a great video on YouTube from the Blogger Help group that should get you up and running (tinyurl.com/qgokg6).

If the podcasting bug bites hard and you start creating regular "shows," don't forget to go to the various directories to get yourself listed. Start with iTunes by clicking on the Podcast link on the iTunes homepage and then clicking on the "Submit a Podcast" icon that appears on the next page. Podcastalley.com and EPNweb.org are a couple others you might want to register with as well.

Now, if all of this still seems like too much work, you might want to check out a couple of Web-based podcasting services that make things even easier. The aptly named Podomatic.com is my favorite, but Odeo.com does pretty much the same thing. Create an account at Podomatic, and once you are logged in, click on the "My Podcast" link. Then click on "Post an Episode," and on the next page, fill out the basic information in the form and then click "Record" at the bottom. Podomatic will find your microphone, and once it does, you can record your podcast directly onto its server. (Remember, however, you can't edit what you record, so you might need to redo it a few times until you get it right.) It will even set you up with your own iTunes subscribe-able blog where you can send people to listen to your work.

And with that, you and your students should be well on your way to fame and, well, fame in amateur radio.

Video Publishing

While elementary school kids seem to love podcasting, older kids have started gravitating to video in a big way. And the biggest reason for that without question is YouTube.com. Bought by Google back in 2006 for over a billion dollars, YouTube is already having an enormous disruptive effect on our society, and it's also becoming a place where more and more of our students go to publish the artifacts of their lives. As of this writing, over 20 hours of videos are being uploaded to YouTube every minute, which translates to almost four years' worth of video uploaded each day (tinyurl.com/p464gl). Staggering numbers, if you ask me.

Not surprisingly, it's also a site that most schools have chosen to block. While, as with the other sites we've discussed here, the vast majority of YouTube content is appropriate, the "anyone can publish anything" aspect can be unsettling. (Still, wouldn't it be better to teach students how to deal with less-than-salient content that they see when they get home?) The same goes for Google Video and a number of the other popular uploading sites. So, a number of alternatives for educators are already springing up, the most notable of which is TeacherTube.com. TeacherTube has thousands of student-and-teacher-produced videos and wants yours as well.

The great part about these online services is that they're free, number one, and they are unlimited in terms of their use. And, in the case of YouTube, you can even record video right from your computer onto their server. Very cool. But as with podcasting, there is a certain amount of writing and preparation that goes into great movie making. It's digital storytelling in its most complex form, and it requires a significant amount of thinking and work to do it well. And, of course, the process is a bit more complex, making it difficult to cover in this small amount of space. My goal here is to point you in the right direction to get started.

If you want some ideas of what can be done, one of the masters of student video is Marco Torres, a social studies teacher at San Fernando High School in California. Over the past seven years, he's had hundreds of students producing and publishing video both online and at the local "ICan

Festival de Cine" (tinyurl.com/6aalqr). I would definitely urge you to spend a little time watching some of their efforts because they represent some of the best examples of student cinema video I've seen. And if you do take the time, you'll notice that every one of the videos that Marco's kids produces has a meaning beyond the classroom. These are done for real purposes, for real audiences, and are a great reminder as to the potential of the Read/Write Web. (My personal favorite is "Parents" at tinyurl.com/qqg4kg.)

Getting started with video requires a bit more of an investment than with podcasting, but you can still produce some great movies on a shoestring budget. And remember, while quality is important, what's critical are the writing, producing, and publishing skills that students learn in the process. In that regard, the time investment is also much greater.

Digital video cameras can run into the thousands of dollars these days, but you should be able to find a decent one for $300 or less. (A good starting point for your search is at cNet.com.) If there is one requirement for whatever you choose, make sure the camera has an external input for a microphone. That way, if you are shooting video from across the room, you can buy an extra long (like 30 feet) mic extension cord and drape it over a broomstick to create a makeshift boom mic for better audio quality.

Before filming, remember to take the time to have students plan their movies using storyboards that frame out the story, and to do some basic instruction on how to hold and use the camera. One of the best resources for this that I've found is the video podcast at IzzyVideo.com. Just check out the list along the right hand side of the page and you'll see a list of the dozens of short tutorials that can really help you understand the nuances of digital video production.

Once you have a camera, and you've shot some video, you'll need to do some editing and production. Luckily, both Windows and Mac platforms have good basic video editors in MovieMaker and iMovie, respectively. Both allow you to import video and audio, and you can record audio voiceovers right onto your movie as well. You can create title screens, add text, run credits, and much more. In fact, the capabilities of these two free programs will most likely far outpace your and your students' needs. Both come with pretty good "Getting Started" tutorials that I urge you to check out, or, of course, there are entire books out there dedicated to the subject.

And, no surprise, there are also online video recording and editing alternatives. (Have I mentioned that the Web is becoming an app?) One to look at from an easy recording standpoint is JayCut.com, where you can upload your raw video from your computer, mix files together, add music and audio, and publish to your favorite video site. There are already many alternatives out there, so you may want to dig around your network for some suggestions when you read this.

Once again, the part about all of this that I love the most is that whatever you and your students create can be shared widely. And to me, that just changes the whole equation. To quote Marco Torres, these videos "should have wings" and be created for real audiences outside the classroom. Again, if you can't use YouTube as a video repository, try TeacherTube. Just create a free account and use the very easy upload process to get your videos online. And once they are there, take the equally handy-dandy embed code provided and add your video right to your blog by copying and pasting the HTML code into your blog's post-editing form. (Remember, you need to be in HTML editing mode to make it work.)

And one last thing you can do in terms of distributing what you create—make it a video podcast. With iTunes, it is pretty painless to take your creation and turn it into an MP4 file that can then be put on an iPod for viewing wherever you may be. First, click on the "Movies" section under your library in iTunes. Then, from the "File" menu, select "Import" and browse to whatever file you want to bring into your library. Once it's in there, just click on it once to highlight it and then go to the "Advanced" menu and select "Convert Selection for iPod." In a few minutes, depending on the size of your movie, you'll have a mini version that will synch right up with your iPod, or can be posted somewhere else for your students to download to their own devices or for others to subscribe to as they would any other podcast (see above).

SCREENCASTING

One step up from podcasting is screencasting, which is a relatively new medium that I think has a lot of promise in the classroom. Simply put, screencasting involves capturing what you or your students do on the computer with an audio narration to go with it. The easiest way to understand screencasting is to watch one. So, right now, go watch one of my all-time favorite screencasts about Wikipedia that was done by John Udell at tinyurl.com/ydp2sfg. I'll wait until you come back.

Okay, get the picture? (And "get" Wikipedia a bit more?) The potential is pretty obvious, I think. From a teaching standpoint, you could create screencasts as support materials when teaching complex skills on the computer. If you had a Tablet PC, you could capture the ink annotations or written solutions that you share with your students. You could create training videos for peers, narrate PowerPoint-created tours for parents, or make video collections of exemplary student work. Once again, the possibilities are enormous.

With your students, you could ask them to annotate their work in voice as they show it on screen. Or, you could have them create their own Internet tours. Or, have them read stories or poetry they write with accompanying visuals they have either created or found. They can even take some of those podcast ideas and attach visual images to go along with it. It's limited only by your and their creativity.

The best part? It's so easy to do. If you can podcast, you can screencast. But, obviously, screencasting takes a bit more preparation. You're combining audio with video, which means you need to think more carefully about what you want to do and how best to do it. You'll need to prepare what it is you want to show on the computer and you'll probably want to create at least an outline of a script. You might even want to create a storyboard that sketches out the visual and the audio together. No matter how you plan, it's not a bad idea to run through it a couple of times before actually starting to create the screencast.

There are a lot of different screencasting tools to choose from these days, but from an ease-of-use standpoint, I love Jing (Jingproject.com, see Figure 8.4). At this writing, it's a free download that works on either a Mac or a Windows machine, and it's one of the easiest pieces of software to use that I've found in a long time.

Figure 8.4 When you click the video button in Jing, you get a three-second countdown to when the recording function begins.

Once you have Jing up and running, it sits in the upper right-hand corner of your screen like a small sun, waiting and ready. Any time you want to make a quick capture, you just mouse over it and three rays of sunlight shoot out—a plus-sign icon that let's you start the capture process, a disk icon that lets you look at the history of what you have captured, and a gear icon where you can configure things. Click on the plus sign and you get crosshairs that you can drag over any portion of the screen that you want to capture. If you want the entire window, just drag the crosshairs onto it and click once. When you are done selecting, just click on the "video" tab at the bottom left, and you'll get a 3 . . . 2 . . . 1 countdown to begin your recording. (You can also use Jing as a screen-capture tool by clicking on the "Image" tab instead.)

At this point, start talking and working on your desktop to capture whatever process you're demonstrating. Remember that most screencasts should be shorter rather than longer, and, in fact, Jing limits you to five minutes. When you're done, click "Stop." (You can also click "Pause" if you need to stop just for a moment.) Immediately, Jing will pop up a playback window where you can preview what you just captured. Take a look, and if you don't like it, just cancel it and do it again.

If you do like the end result, here is where Jing makes things really, really easy. To save it, just click on the word "File" below the preview and then click the "Share" icon. Follow the instructions to let Jing know where you want your screencasts saved on your hard drive. (It saves as an .swf file, by the way.) If you want your video to be saved directly to the Web, click on "Screencast.com" instead of file, and your screencast will automatically be uploaded to your account, which you'll set up during the registration process. (Right now, you get 200 MB of free space at Screencast.com to play with, and an annual unlimited account is about $40.00.) If you want to share directly to YouTube, you can configure Jing to do that as well. (And remember, Jing works with Flickr, too.) When it's finished, all you need to do to share your screencast with the world is to distribute the URL, which, by the way, automatically gets pasted to your clipboard when the upload is finished. It's almost too easy.

Last but certainly not least, you can embed your screencast on your blog or wiki by going to your Screencast.com account page and copying the code provided there. Just paste it into the HTML editor for whatever page you want to add it to (like your class or school homepage, perhaps?) and anyone who visits will be able to play it right there and then.

LIVE STREAMING—WEB TV FOR THE CLASSROOMS

The most recent entry into the multimedia publishing discussion is live-streaming video to the Web. In a nutshell, we're talking the ability of teachers and students to create their own TV shows online in just a few clicks. And, if you have a personal learning network at your disposal, you also have a potential audience at your fingertips.

While this is still pretty unexplored territory in education circles, and while the tools are evolving rapidly, a surprisingly large number of teachers are already experimenting with the idea of creating live "television" with their students in their classrooms and schools. And because of how incredibly easy it is to do this, that number is increasing greatly every day.

The examples run the gamut: school plays and musicals being broadcast to relatives far and wide, student science presentations for parents to watch, live student-run daily news broadcasts, live teacher professional development that anyone can tune into, conference workshops and presentations free to those who couldn't make the trip, and all sorts of other possibilities. Basically, we're close to the point where every school, every classroom, every person, in fact, can own a television station.

Don't believe me? Here's a quick story. On the night of the New Hampshire primary in 2008, I got a Skypechat asking me to come watch and participate in a live review of the election returns on the "Newly Ancient" streaming TV channel at Ustream.tv. So I clicked on the link, and who should I find conducting a careful analysis of the voting while talking live via Skype with people around the world and interacting with about 15 "viewers" in the show's chat room but Arthus Erea, that 14-year old blogger I mentioned a couple of chapters back. That was a "sit up and take notice" moment for me, no doubt.

How do you do it? See Figure 8.5—the requirements are a fast (or pretty fast) and stable Internet connection, a computer with a microphone and either an external Webcam or built-in video camera, a free account at an online video streaming site, and an idea. If you have those ingredients, you can be streaming live to the net in under five minutes. Really.

Right now, the online video streaming site of choice among those in my network is at Ustream.tv, a free site that not only makes streaming easy but offers a chat room for viewers to interact with while watching, archives your shows for later viewing, and, among other features appealing to educators, allows you to password protect your show so only those who you share the login with can view the live stream. You can sign up for a free UStream account by simply clicking through the "Sign Up" process at the top right of the page. Once finished, click on the "MyShows" tab, give your show a name, and then, if you are set up and ready to go, click "Start Broadcasting" (see Figure 8.6, page 128). (If you're not ready, just save your show until you are.) You can also come back and work your way through the various configuration tabs to create a unique look for your show, to get code to embed the show into your school homepage, for instance, and to determine who can view

Figure 8.5 The UStream broadcast page shows the live stream on the left and has a chat area for viewers' comments and reactions on the right. It also lists thumbnails for all of the archived shows.

your show and play in the chat room. (The password option is under the "Advanced" tab, by the way.)

When you click "Broadcast Now," a "Local Broadcasting Widget" box will pop up and load the production tools. You will be asked to approve the use of your microphone and webcam, and, once you do, you will see what will be broadcast and you'll be able to adjust the levels of your microphone as well. Once everything is adjusted, click "Start Broadcast" a final time, and, if you want to archive the session, click "Start Recording" as well. (Recording allows you to save any show under an hour to your computer and to use the embed code on the show page to make it play on your blog or wiki or whatever. Note, however, that the chat conversation does not record—you have to copy and paste that into a document at regular intervals if you want to save it.)

Figure 8.6   When you click "Start Broadcast" on your UStream page, you will be asked to "allow" the use of your Webcam and microphone.

Now, you need to let your audience know that you're "on air." Obviously, you should plan ahead by communicating the Web address of your show and the time you will be broadcasting. Your Web address can be found under the "Share" tab after you click on "My Shows" once you are logged in. (It will look something like "ustream.tv/channel/weblogg-ed-tv.") But the other way to get an instant audience is to use your network. (Hopefully, you're well on your way to creating that by now.) And the easiest way to shout out your show to the network is by using Twitter. Just send a "tweet" with the show address, and folks will be showing up in droves before you know it.

A lot of presenters (myself included) stream many of their presentations and take advantage of the chat feature that Ustream provides. The "backchannel" conversation can be a great way of interacting with the online audience and broadening the scope of the dialogue. And some classrooms are really starting to take advantage of live streaming. On fifth-grade teacher Bill Chamberlain's class blog (tinyurl.com/clby52) from Noel, Missouri, you can see a live stream of his classroom whenever it's in session, and on his Ustream page (tinyurl.com/69aesr) you can find archives of presentations, projects, and all sorts of other stuff. It's a great repository of student work and learning.

On last note for Mac users. If you are going to play with streaming video, you need to get CamTwist (tinyurl.com/33ckvz), a free download that creates all sorts of production possibilities including adding slide shows, videos, music, multiple cameras, text scrolls, and more. As of this writing, there is nothing like it for Windows machines—sorry.

And just when you thought live streaming couldn't get any easier, guess what? You can now do on-the-spot, live, interactive video reporting using your phone. That's right. Your phone. Let's take a moment, shall we, to consider the implications of that little development when in comes to our kids. Done shuddering yet? While the prospect may seem a bit unsettling, to put in mildly, to me it's just another reason why we have to get our brains around these shifts and be able to teach our kids the ethics and sensibilities to make good choices regarding these powerful technologies they are carrying in their pockets.

No question, the live streaming from the phone option is not as high quality as from the computer, but, in all honesty, it isn't bad. At this moment, Ustream Mobile works with just about any Nokia phone that has a camera, and with a jail-broken iPhone 3G. (I never told you that, by the way.) You simply download the application to your phone, find something worthwhile to stream (like my daughter's basketball games), and press whatever button means "Start" on your phone. Anyone who has the address of your Ustream.tv "show" can just tune in and watch. Like the computer version, you can save the recordings to your show page, and, whenever anyone watching your show types in a chat comment or question, you see it on the video screen on your phone so you can just talk back a reply. Pretty amazing.

Also going down this road is Qik.com, which, at this moment at least, supports even more phones. And if you do have a jail-broken iPhone 3G (shhhh!), both services now have apps in the App Store on iTunes. (Ustream also has an app that allows you to watch live streams on your iPhone, regardless of whether you've hacked it or not.)

All of that being said, our ability to create and share multimedia in more and more transparent ways is only going to continue to expand. The potentials are huge, and the pitfalls challenging. But publishing to an audience can be a great motivator for students. Podcasting, videocasting, screencasting, and now live-streaming TV are all great ways to get student content online.

9 Social Networks

Facebook, Ning, Connections, and Communities

O ne of the most important pieces of reading from November of 2008 was a report titled "Living and Learning With New Media" that was released by the MacArthur Foundation and the Digital Youth Project (Ito et al., 2008). It details the results of a three-year study that examined "young people's participation in the new media ecology." Simply put, I think it's a must read for anyone interested in understanding the lives of kids in these new, connected spaces. A key finding in the study was this: Our kids are using social networking technologies in two important ways. First, they engage in what the report calls "friendship-based ways," which most adults are familiar with. These uses help kids stay connected to the people who they know in their physical spaces—their friends at school, the people they meet at summer camp, or their teammates, among others. I'm reminded of this every time I get stuck behind a school bus coming home and see students stepping off onto their driveways intently staring at their phones as they text the friend who was probably sitting next to them on the bus.

But the other way that youth are beginning to connect using these tools is more compelling. That is, kids are using social networks to "explore interests and find information that goes beyond what they have access to at school or in their local community" (Ito et al., 2008). And in these "interest-based" interactions, they are connecting to peers and adults outside of their physical spaces, people who they don't know but with whom they share a passion. They become at once teachers and learners in these spaces, and, in the process, they learn about the things that school can't or won't teach them. In both of these interactions, whether friendship based or interest based, the study found that kids engage in "self-directed, peer-based learning" that looks very different from most of their experiences in school.

There's little question that therein lies the amazing appeal of the technologies that we've been talking about in this book, this ability to connect and learn with others around the things we really care about learning. (Sounds familiar by now, I hope.) And there's also little doubt that that ability also complicates what we do as educators a great deal. At some point, we're going to have to get our brains around what it means to participate in an online community or "social network" the way our kids are beginning to do if we really want to help them do it well.

From the friendship-based and interest-based perspectives, there are some ready-made sites and tools out there to help us, namely Facebook.com for the former and Ning.com for the latter. Both make group forming around the people we know or the interests we pursue almost too easy. But from an educational standpoint, they also pose a unique set of problems and challenges for classroom use, ones that can be fairly well overcome, as always, through a combination of personal experience, communication, instruction, and good policy. (I put "personal experience" first for a reason, by the way.)

If you don't think there's anything to this social networking thing, read on. For Facebook, the site that was started in a Harvard dorm room in 2004, the numbers are, in a word, staggering. At the beginning of July 2009, Facebook was growing by an amazing 700,000 accounts *per day,* and its total membership was close to 250 million (making it the fourth-largest country in the world were it a physical place) (Smith, 2009). But here is the real kicker: The fastest growing segment of Facebook users today is the over-55 set, meaning parents and grandparents are finally starting to figure out what all the fuss is about. (That of course means that Facebook will soon be anathema to all of our students—we can only guess where they'll go next.)

In terms of Ning, a site that lets you create your own personal Facebook-like network around whatever your specific interest is, the numbers are equally impressive. The service, which launched in 2005, has hosted over 1.5 million networks at this writing, and it's adding them at about half a million a year. Now, like Facebook's numbers, not all of those are active accounts, but as of last April it had over 6 million active users on those sites, a number that continues steadily upward (Lardinois, 2009). And while Facebook does allow for some "interest-based" connections, there are some seriously powerful examples of groups coming together in Ning sites to do great work and great learning together.

The key to both of these sites for educators is to move beyond the friendship-based connections and really explore the potentials of the networked, interest-based learning that's possible within these frames. They are places where sharing and collaboration and even collective action (in Clay Shirky's words) can take place in some profound ways, and they are spaces that might allow us to change the way we think about those things in the context of a much different, connected world. I love what last year's Humanities, Arts, Sciences and Technology Advanced Collaboratory study on "The Future of Learning Institutions in a Digital Age" had to say about the way we might reframe our concept of working together in the classroom (tinyurl.com/n4d4dh).

Learning has traditionally assumed a winner-take-all competitive form rather than a cooperative form. One cooperates in a classroom only if it maximizes narrow self-interest. Networked learning, in contrast, is committed to a vision of the social that stresses cooperation, interactivity, mutual benefit, and social engagement. The power of ten working interactively will invariably outstrip the power of one looking to beat out the other nine.

Frankly, connecting online or digitally with people we already know is pretty easy these days. Actually doing something together with them to learn or to make the world a better place is another story altogether. We can see it writ large at sites like Kiva.org, which allows us to provide microloans to those less fortunate, or TakingItGlobal.org, a social network that "connects you to the social issues that affect us all." Both of those sites make it easy to do good work in collaborative ways with other people and to learn a great deal in the process. The potential power of Facebook and Ning for educators, however, is that they allow us to personalize those potentials in the context of our own students and our own curriculum. In the process, we can teach students all sorts of important lessons about digital citizenship, safety, information literacy, and more.

FACEBOOK FOR PERSONAL CONNECTIONS

Facebook, obviously, is a hot-button issue in the K–12 world, enough to cause many a teacher and administrator to throw up his or her hands and ask, "Why bother?" I'm just guessing here, but I'm thinking about 90 percent of public schools block it and would rather it didn't exist. There is no question that there are all sorts of opportunities for our kids to do stupid things there, things that parents might very well blame on us. But if for no other reason, we should bother because Facebook (and MySpace and Bebo and who knows what's to come) has become an important online space in our kids lives, a space that, once again, no one is teaching them how to leverage for learning. And, believe it or not, there is a great deal of learning that occurs and can occur on these social network sites, not just from a "network literacy" standpoint.

I'll get on my soapbox here again for a bit and suggest that whether we like it or not, if we're working with kids in schools (or elsewhere), we have a responsibility to understand what Facebook is all about, even if it's just to the extent that we participate there for ourselves, on our own time, for our own connections. I'm sure, in fact, that few of you are even able to use

Facebook with your students because of district filtering or even pressure from state organizations or local unions. Even more, I've heard plenty of stories of teachers being told that they should not even have a personal Facebook profile because of the potential problems with putting parts of ourselves out there online. As you might guess, I find that appalling. Whatever the challenges that prevent us from making social networking a part of our curriculum, they should not stop us from being able to talk about Facebook or to share or model our own experiences there in appropriate ways so kids at an early age have some context for what the expectations and roles are that await them there. And, even more, no teacher should be denied exploration of a technology that with good pedagogy could be a valuable learning tool for students, or, more importantly, could provide important context for learning in general.

That being said, the instances of K–12 classrooms or schools using Facebook are still few and far between. The couple of examples that I'll show you later are representative of what relatively little is out there right now. But let me stress, my goal here is not so much to encourage you to bring social networking a la Facebook into your classroom as much as it is to bring it into your own personal practice. Not that you need it, but you hereby have my permission not to think too hard about your students or your classrooms or your schools here. Just focus on what you can learn from these types of connections and spaces that can inform your own learning.

From a personal, friendship-based-connections standpoint, signing up for a Facebook account is pretty straightforward. Just go to Facebook.com (Figure 9.1), fill out the form on the homepage, click on the link in the confirmation e-mail, and start finding friends to connect with. If you want, Facebook will scour your e-mail account to see who else might already be signed up. (This could be a good or bad thing.) Make sure to fill out your profile and add your picture so others can potentially find you. Remember, you can choose not to accept friend requests as they come in. And, without getting too deeply into the psychology of "friending," a topic that you can spend days reading and agonizing over, it's perfectly okay to leave some requests unanswered. (Note: Facebook offers a number of different levels of transparency that you might want to explore, and they are covered in great detail in the "Teacher's Guide to Using Facebook" by Bernadette Rego, which can be found at tinyurl.com/12yheq.)

To start searching for people who you might know, just click on "Friends" at the top of the page and then select "Find Friends" from the drop-down list. Use the "Search for People" form to start adding names of old high school friends, colleagues, former girlfriends or boyfriends, or even (gasp!) relatives. You may have to do some digging around because by this point there is hardly a unique name left to search for in the Facebook database.

Figure 9.1 Facebook is the largest social network in the world, adding over 700,000 people per day.

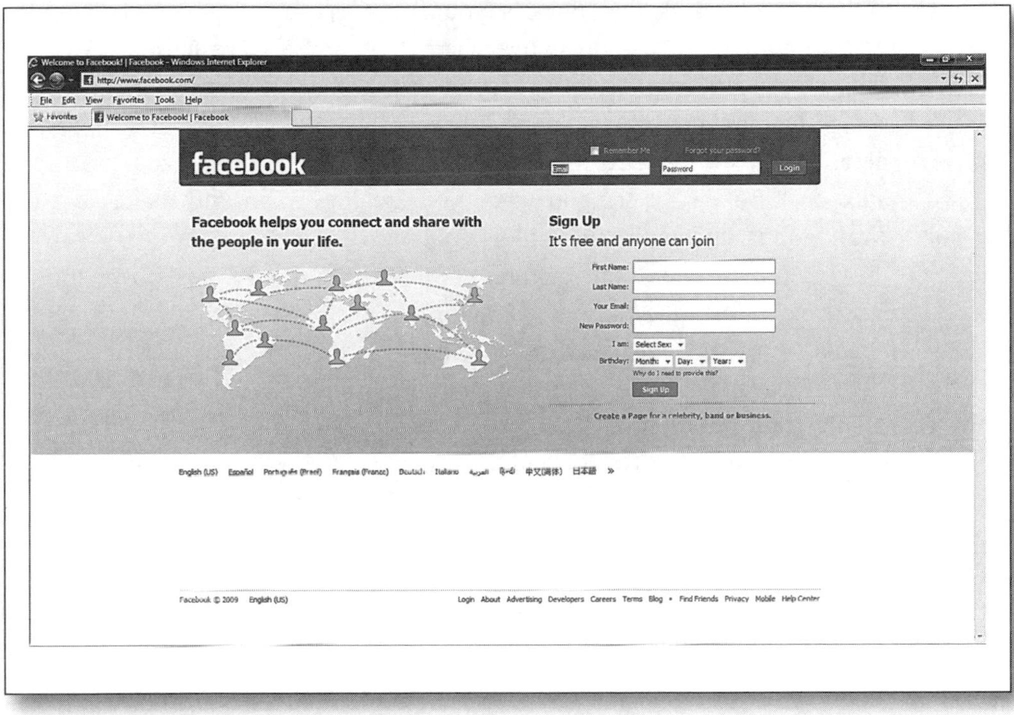

Once you do find someone you know, just click "Add as Friend" and that person will be sent a friend request asking to approve you. (Keep your fingers crossed.)

When you "friend" someone, what that means is that their updates will appear on your Facebook homepage. Just click the "Home" button at the top of the page when you are logged in. Understand that Facebook now aggregates a lot of the content your "friends" may be posting elsewhere like Twitter or their blogs, so what you'll see may be more of a "life stream," as some are calling it, rather than updates into Facebook. Or not. Some people I know use Facebook pretty exclusively as the place they update their lives and post online. It all depends on taste.

Either way, for those who have "friended" you to see what you're up to, you're going to have to post some updates. You do that by filling in the "What's on your mind?" blank at the top of the updates column. Here you can wax philosophic about breakfast, post a picture of your lovable little puppy, add a video you found on YouTube, or pick apart the latest blog post you read about the merits of NCLB. Just remember that whatever you post there, your "friends" will see it. And what they do with it is anyone's guess. (I have mentioned, haven't I, that nothing, I repeat, nothing is guaranteed to be private on the Web.)

Now, you can also leave messages to your individual friends by writing on their "wall." To do that, click on your friend's name and then enter a greeting (or photo, or video, and so on) where it says "Write Something." You can also use your friends' walls as ways to find other people to connect to or engage in some conversations around what interesting topics may be posted there. If you want to see what people have been writing on your wall, just click on "Profile" at the top when you are logged in and make sure the "Wall" tab is selected in the middle column.

One quick note about pictures. Whenever someone posts a picture to Facebook, he has the option of "tagging" the people in the picture, which means the picture is automatically added to the "tagged" person's photo album. That means that even though you may not have posted that embarrassing Halloween photo from five years ago, someone who has a copy of that photo could do just that and tag you with it. I tell you this not to scare you further away from using Facebook, but to make sure you understand what types of interactions our students are dealing with here. Figuring out how you will deal with these realities will go a long way toward helping you mentor your students through their own use.

FACEBOOK IN THE CLASSROOM

Obviously, we could go on for pages (entire books, in fact) on all of the other things that you can do with Facebook. You'll have to explore and learn on your own, perhaps even get answers from your social network as you become more and more of a "networked" learner. But I do want to touch on the ways in which you might think about using it in your classroom should the opportunity present itself and should you think it's the right technology for whatever it is you want to teach.

Some general advice to start—while some teachers don't seem to have any qualms about "friending" their students, I would advise against it. Make it clear to your classes that your use of Facebook is "interest-based" not "friendship-based," and make sure you articulate your reasons for choosing Facebook as a networking space. Articulate those same reasons to your supervisor and your principal to make sure your efforts are supported, and make sure the parents of your students are all on board as well. If you can't make the compelling case for using Facebook to their satisfaction, you may want to spend a little more time experimenting for yourself. Finally, when your group is up and running, share your story, good or bad, with your colleagues—both at your school and to those of us who are following from afar. We have a lot to learn as well.

Most uses of Facebook by teachers are grounded in the creation of either public but usually private groups on the site where classes can exchange information, write on each other's walls, answer questions, and create a shared space of materials for the course. (There is an add on to Facebook called "Courses" that you might want to explore as well.) To create a group, just go to tinyurl.com/ldq867 and go through the easy setup process. (You need to be logged in, of course.) Once you add the basic information about your group on the first page, the second page allows you to set the transparency. Most teachers go with a "closed" group, which means the front page is open to view, but all photos and discussions and everything else are open to members only. (You can even make a "secret" group if you really want to pull the curtain closed. Other options on the page allow administrators to control who can add links, photos, and videos. Inviting students to the group from the next page is easy as long as you have an e-mail address for each. Remember that to get back to your group page you can always click on the link that will appear under your "Profile" on the "Info" tab. As always, if you struggle, odds are pretty good that you can turn to one of your more trusted students to help.

So let's look at a couple ways that teachers and schools are beginning to dabble in the Facebook universe. (See Figures 9.2 and 9.3.)

Jim Meredith, a Catholic school social studies teacher in Philadelphia, was looking for a way to engage his students more fully in his curriculum and thought Facebook might be the answer. "When I mentioned Facebook, it caused a massive buzz in the room," Jim says. "Every one of them already had their own accounts. They were so enthusiastic, and I knew the die had been cast" (J. Meredith, personal communication, July 7, 2009).

He decided to create a totally private site for his class, and after some discussions with the technology coordinator, the Archdiocese agreed to unblock Facebook from his office and classroom computers (upon request). Jim began by holding two class sessions dedicated to Internet use and appropriateness. Afterward, each Monday Jim posted a discussion board topic to which each student had to post a response by the following Friday. He told them that the "wall" was their space to post any appropriate material that they thought would add to the class discussions, and they quickly began to add relevant photos and videos. It all worked about as well as he could have hoped.

"The unintended consequence of our private group is that it built a strong class community," Jim says. "Quiet kids in class spoke up online, and when we had a student who had a serious health issue in the spring, the class used the group to lift her up and keep her informed" (J. Meredith, personal communication, July 7, 2009).

In fact, students asked to keep the Facebook group going after the course ended. While he's not sure whether or not Facebook was the reason, course enrollment for the fall of 2009 jumped from 14 to 26, and Jim plans to create

> **Figure 9.2** An AP U.S. Government and Politics class on Facebook: Archbishop Ryan AP U.S. Government and Politics (tinyurl.com/kkabum)

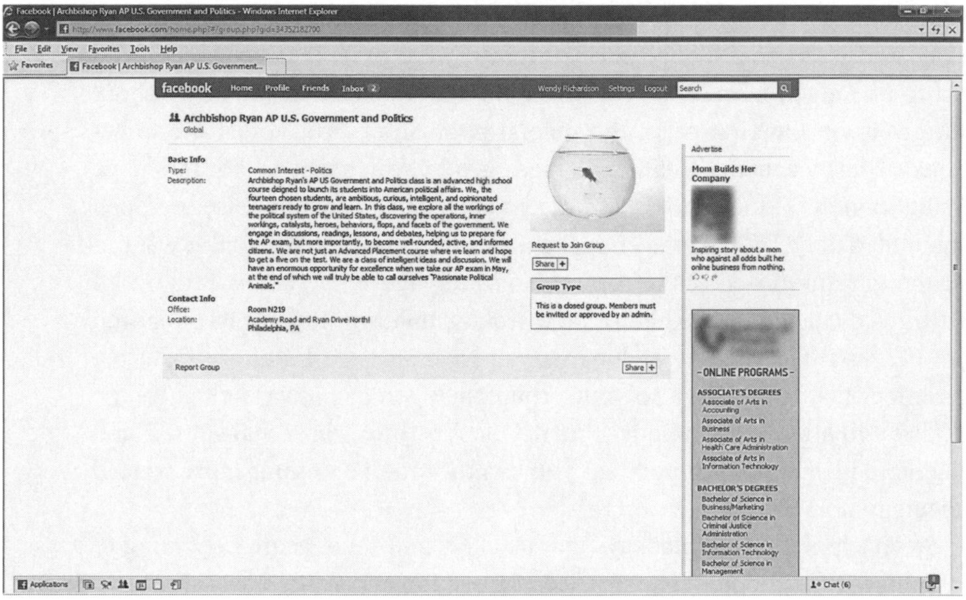

new groups for that new class as well as for a freshman World History class. As Jim says, he's using Facebook "educationally, appropriately, and ethically IN the classroom."

The Unquiet Library: Creekview High School Media Center (tinyurl.com/1956sc)

Creekview High, in Canton, Georgia, probably has one of the most active K–12 library sites on Facebook. It's a totally public site that serves as a portal for news about books, links to interesting articles, photos about library events, and much more. Teacher librarians Buffy Hamilton and Ruth Fleet have made the site a part of a large lineup of social media, including a library blog and wiki, Delicious bookmarks, Twitter account, Flickr photos, even its own YouTube channel. (Get links to all of those components at tinyurl.com/15xy3j.) It's a great example of how all of these tools can be integrated.

On the Facebook page, students can get information on new books, links to interesting articles that deal with reading or technology or social media, photos of events, and links to interviews with authors. It's a running stream of news and events that's easily accessible to the millions who use Facebook. But even more, the site serves as a great meeting point for librarians from all over the world who want to share ideas and give feedback.

The key is that social media is a part of the lives of the librarians who run the site. "I try to model these values in my practice as I am constantly tapping into my personal learning network for strategies and ideas to help my students and teachers tap into the power of the dizzying changes in the information landscape," says Hamilton (cited in Valenza, 2009).

Figure 9.3   The Unquiet Library: Creekview High School Media Center

A NING FOR ALL PASSIONS

Despite the continued explosion of Facebook's popularity, it's still not a site that many K–12 schools allow through their filters. (MySpace rarely makes the cut either.) But if you want a Facebook-like environment to deliver some of your curriculum and teach some social networking skills as well, there is an alternative: Ning.com.

Briefly, Ning allows you to create your own free social networking site around whatever topic you want, complete with personal profiles, photos, video links, groups, discussions, blogs, and more. (We'll dig into those details in a bit.) For educators, the best part about a Ning site is that it's totally self-contained—meaning all of that sharing and posting happens under one roof, and it can be totally private only to those whom you want to participate. Teachers who create Ning sites have total administrative control over who can gain access to the site and, to some degree, the extent of their participation there.

You can do a great deal from a classroom perspective with Ning. It's a great environment for students to test out their writing skills for a dedicated audience, and the many ways in which members can comment and interact provide some great opportunities to discuss the ethics and safety that go along with connecting online. Class portfolios are almost a natural outgrowth of long-term Ning use as students add their best practice artifacts, and it can be a great place to collect and link to resources on the Web.

While there aren't a lot of downsides to Ning, it's not perfect. First, you can't share individual blog posts or other artifacts publicly; the site you create is either all private or all public. (You can, however, make it so the site is public but only approved members can change it, must like the "public" setting on wikis we discussed a couple of chapters back.) Second, the Ning interface can get a bit overwhelming as more and more content gets added. There are lots of different apps that you can drop into your profile page, for instance, everything from games to music players to photo editors. It doesn't take long for the navigation to get confusing, so think carefully (and teach your kids to do the same) when adding elements. Third, like Facebook, the Ning terms of service restricts the use of the sites to members that are over the age of 13, which means this is primarily a tool for seventh through twelfth graders. Fourth, if you do set up a private Ning, you lose the ability to subscribe to RSS feeds coming out of the site. Finally, unless you go through the process of requesting they are removed from your education-related site, Google Ads will appear on the homepage. (You'll find the step-by-step process of requesting removal at tinyurl.com/5d8tca.)

Despite all of that, Ning sites are cropping up just about everywhere online, and that includes a great many dedicated to education. You'll find a long list of them on the Social Networks in Education wiki (tinyurl.com/2qu8p8). Many of these sites are being used to connect teachers around their own interests and passions, and the number of members of such sites range from a couple of dozen to over a couple of thousand. The mother of them all is Classroom20.com, a Ning site that was started by educator/consultant Steve Hargadon just two years ago that at this writing has attracted over 25,000 members from around the globe. While all of those folks aren't currently active on the site, a normal day can see upward of 100 interactions, everything from posting to individual blogs, scheduling events, and viewing videos. Discussions on the site are organized by different tools, curricular subjects, or areas of conversation, such as "administration" or "gifted" or "parents," for example. There's a connection to be made here for just about any educator, providing they don't get too overwhelmed by the scale.

One step down in size from Classroom20 and one step up in focus is the "English Companion Ning" (tinyurl.com/8g7xu3) where about 5,000 or so English teacher types share ideas and experiences about teaching with technology, poetry round tables, writing portfolios, and more. It's a pretty vibrant, cooperative space. (A quick search will find you a Ning for every discipline, by the way, as well as every passion. I especially like the Book Marketing Ning for, um, obvious reasons. As always, be careful what you search for, as not all Nings are as upstanding as the ones cited here.)

For a smaller, more focused, "community" feel, you might try the "Seedlings" Ning site (tinyurl.com/mamt3r), which was created for listeners of the bimonthly "Seedlings Podcast" hosted by Maine educators Bob Sprankle, Cheryl Oakes, and Alice Barr. With a little over 300 members, you get a real sense of community, of folks genuinely interested in one another and the topics they are exploring. Not that that doesn't happen on the larger sites, but it's especially apparent here. (And, besides that, the Seedlings Ning is just plain old pretty in its design.)

NING IN THE CLASSROOM

It shouldn't be too hard here to see the potential for Ning sites in the classroom or for a school community. In fact, a lot of teachers and administrators are already pretty far down the road to making Ning a valued part of their practice, including not just students and teachers but parents and community members as well. Here are a few examples of what Nings can do.

The ISA Internship Program—Ms. Moorman's Virtual Classroom (tinyurl.com/lv6qm7)

The International School of the Americas in San Antonio has every student do a 120-hour "career exploration" internship before graduation, and in fall of 2008, teacher Honor Moorman stepped into the coordinator position. Her first question was how to bring together all of these students each working in different places with different schedules so they could share experiences, reflect on their work, and support one another in the process. The obvious answer? Ning.

The ISA Internship Ning had two goals at its inception. First, Honor was "trying to create a virtual classroom . . . where students could converse and collaborate, and where I could support and enrich their learning. Second, I was hoping to enhance the Internship curriculum in a way that would help prepare students for the literacy demands of the twenty-first century" (Moorman, 2009, p. 6). To her credit, she spent a great deal of time preparing students for this work by discussing the potentials and pitfalls of social networking in education, and she even co-constructed a separate Acceptable Use Policy for the site with her students. Even so, it took some time for students to warm up to the site, as many of them saw it as time away from their more friendship-based connections.

What you'll see on the site's homepage (which is open to the public) is a pretty regular thread of blog posts and discussions that speak to the challenges and excitement that internships of this type can bring. Students gather in groups around their specific areas of interest, and there is a great mix of the social connections that these networks facilitate and also the learning that can happen when a group of students with a similar focus begins to exchange ideas in an online space.

St. Joe H20 (tinyurl.com/ldgwkb)

Sean Nash set up his Ning for his Marine Biology students in St. Josephs, Missouri, two years ago to build conversations about the subject and to invite experts in from places that were actually near an ocean. One such expert, author Osha Gray Davidson, became an integral part of the class discussion, at one point even sending a 350-million-year-old piece of coral to one of Sean's students who had written compellingly about endangered coral species on his Ning blog. The results of these types of interactions have been remarkable.

"Current and future students now see our site as a living community that connects former and future students as well as a growing lists of experts in the field," Sean writes. "No longer do our students feel like they are in a one-way relationship with a textbook, or a two-way relationship with their teacher. They see the site as a hub of communication that connects the best parts of the past with the growing future of our program" (S. Nash, personal communication, July 10, 2009).

The students use the discussion forums to ask and answer questions, the blogs to reflect on their reading, and they add value to the site by sharing photos or videos they find that are relevant to their learning about marine biology. And in doing so, they've created a real sense of community. It's changed the way Sean approaches his own practice.

"Now my students never really "leave" our program; they are all just a click away from future interactions in a way that moves us together forward as a learning community," Sean says. "I love the ability to 'steer' less and 'suggest' more as a classroom teacher. This tool helps me to feel empowered as a leader of student learning and less as a solitary sage dispensing knowledge" (S. Nash, personal communication, July 10, 2009).

The best part? The entire Ning is public, so you can explore it on your own. Sean has taken great measures to teach his students how to comport themselves in a public space. "We work in public for a reason," Sean says.

ArtSnacks (tinyurl.com/yvmcjh)

So what if you want to start a Ning to connect kids and teachers from around the world around a particular idea or passion? Well, that's exactly what Kansas teacher Kevin Honeycutt has done with the ArtSnacks Ning site. An early member of the Classroom20 community, Kevin decided two years ago to create a site that would allow teachers and kids to work together to create art. The first step after creating the site was to video about 100 mini lessons on drawing various animals, symbols, historical places, and more and make them easily accessible for members to use to draw their own versions and then post those back to the site. "When creating lessons my aim is to integrate vocabulary and standards-based facts into the lessons," Kevin writes (personal communication, July 12, 2009). "I asked teachers to request lessons they needed and to include vocabulary and facts they would like reinforced. For example, when they draw the pond, they hear about ecosystems and the water cycle" (K. Honeycutt, personal communication, July 12, 2009). A great idea, I think.

Today, there are over 2,200 members from over 50 countries on the site who have posted over 11,500 pieces of art for others to view. One of the best parts of the site is that it has about a one-to-one ratio of teachers to students. And as the interest has expanded, so have the offerings. Kids can sign up for live lessons in voice, piano, and guitar through the site by combining Skype and Ustream to create individualized learning channels. Elementary teachers use the network as a center for individual art experiences for their learners and as an extension for curricular concepts. It's even become a place where dropout recovery programs send students for credit recovery.

While it hasn't been easy, Kevin has been amazed with the result. School filters have prevented many teachers and students from taking part, and there's no question that maintaining a "walled garden" site where membership is by request takes time and attention. Still, it has been worth it. "I've been a first-hand witness to the power of social learning networks to foster real, engaged learning," Kevin says. "It's been incredible to watch and be a part of" (personal communication, July 12, 2009).

SETTING UP YOUR NING SITE

It shouldn't come as any surprise at this point that setting up your own personal Ning site is pretty easy. The hard part comes in the management, depending on how many members you admit and the things that you're doing there. As always, I highly suggest you explore Ning's potentials on someone else's site first before flipping the switches on for yourself. With all of the Ning sites for educators talking about their own uses of Ning, you'll get a log of valuable Ning formation and experience in next to no time. And, you'll more easily be able to make the compelling case to the decision makers in your school who do the filtering. So, don't skip that step.

When you're ready, just go to Ning.com and start the creation process by picking a name for your social network and choosing an address. (Remember to think this through carefully just like you did your Blogger address—you can't change it once you choose. Also, don't forget to give this address to the person who runs the filter at your school; in many cases, Ning sites are blocked, but individual sites can be opened up by the address). Next, enter your name, e-mail, set your password, put in your birthday, read the Terms of Service (not) and click "Sign Up." (Remember, you can create as many Ning sites as you like.) On the next page, you get to fill in some more detail. Again, think through the information you add here, even though you will be able to change any or all of it later (even your network name.) And don't worry too much about the public/private option at this point. We'll get back to that in a second.

Now comes the fun part—building the look of your site. As I said earlier, Ning sites can get pretty crowded pretty fast, so I would start with less and build it as you get a feel for the needs of the community. To "add features" just drag and drop the modules on the setup grid. (By the way, if you are good at CSS and HTML, you can create your own personal look later. If you don't know what those stand for, forget I mentioned it.) Personally, I definitely want the "Activity," "Forum," "Members," and "Groups" prominently on my page. You may want to leave the "Photos" and "Video" features but move them to the side. But other than that, I'd start with everything else off the page. (Remember, it's easy to add it all back in later.) Just a reminder: You won't be able to remove the ads from your page at this point. You'll have to contact Ning directly once you're set up and request their removal if you can prove you are an education site. Or you can purchase away the ads for $25 a month.

When you are finished with the form, click "Next" and you'll have the chance to choose a template for your site. Again, if you know some code (or have a geeky 14-year-old in the house), you can customize your look in a lot of ways. But there are over 50 choices available, so you should find at least one to your liking. When you've chosen, click "Launch" and your site is ready to go.

Now here are a couple of things to do right away before you start adding pictures and videos and other content. First, click on "Manage," which will be toward the top somewhere depending on the template you chose. Then find the icon that says "Network Privacy" under the "Your Members" section. There, you want to make your choice as to who can see what and who can join your site. If it were me, I might consider making a public site where visitors can only see the main page and where I approve all new members before they can join. Yeah, I know, that's a bit more work than just locking the whole thing down (as in "Private" for "Only Invited People"). But again, I want my kids to have some public face to their work. (As an aside, going back to Ning's limitations, you might want to keep your site private and publish the best work to a public blog or wiki.)

Remember that despite your best planning and execution, there may be moments when things don't go as you like. A student may post an inappropriate link or add a comment to a post that isn't exactly civil. Worse, a student may bully another or threaten harm. While these instances will be rare if you have been vigilant in your own practice and preparation, you have to plan for their occurrence. Hopefully, if they do happen, they'll be seen as teachable moments and not reasons to shut things down. As Kevin Honeycutt says:

> Sometimes a member can do something less than smart but we eventually catch it. Some people feel that even one negative event on a network is a reason to shut it down, but I would offer that when kids cross behavioral lines in schools, we don't shut them down, we address the issue and try to learn from the experience. In the end, I think we must build online cultures that are self-monitoring. It is obvious to me that this is an area of learning that we must spend time growing. (tinyurl.com/lnbmv5)

When you're done setting the privacy levels, click on the "Feature Controls" icon from the "Manage" page and you'll find a few more switches to flip depending on your needs. Since you created the site, you are the almost all-powerful site administrator, which means you can ban members, delete posts, set profile questions, and all sorts of other fun stuff. Take the time to explore these powers by clicking through the rest of the sections on the "Manage" page.

Before inviting others to your site, you might want to add some content and spruce the place up a bit. You can start by filling out your profile at "My Page." Add a picture and some of your best, most impressive thoughts here. (But whatever you do, don't "Add Apps." If you click on that link, I take no responsibility for what happens to your site or, for that matter, your livelihood.) From your member page you can also add a blog post, start a discussion, add an event, and all sorts of other fun stuff. Again, take some time to kick the tires, so to speak, before you add your students or colleagues or parents or the world to your community.

When you're ready to start entertaining, just click "Invite" and start adding e-mail addresses to the form. (If e-mails are a problem there is a screencast with a very cool workaround with Gmail that will let you create the accounts and set the passwords for distributing to your students. It's at tinyurl.com/lw3s7m.) Remember, once you invite all of your students, you're going to have to approve them as well (depending on how you set things up), so expect some e-mails to come your way pretty fast.

Then, let the connecting and learning begin. Show your students how to set up their own member pages and their blogs, go over commenting and sharing, talk about acceptable and responsible use, start some discussions, and get your community to work. If it's appropriate, invite parents, other teachers, and other classrooms into the mix. And don't forget to reflect on your own learning in the process. But whatever you do, don't let anyone click on that "Add Apps" button.

10 What It All Means

S o, now that you have a good idea of the tools and the pedagogies, what is going to be the impact on education? Obviously, that's a huge question, but it's important to try to put some meaning to the message.

No doubt, the classroom of the Read/Write Web is going to be defined by two unstoppable trends in the use of these technologies. First, with more than 1 trillion pages already on the Web, more and more content both new and old will continue to come online (Alpert & Hajaj, 2008). If you don't believe that, don't forget that Google is currently attempting to scan and digitize more than 50 million books from five of the largest research libraries in the world. In the words of New York Public Library CEO Paul LeClerc, that in itself "is one of the most transformative events in the history of information distribution since Gutenberg" (Graham, 2004). Add to that the desire of Archive.org founder Brewster Kahle to do the same to the 500 million volumes in the Library of Congress, and there is little doubt that the Internet will continue to explode as the most comprehensive source of information in history. As author Thomas Friedman writes in *The World Is Flat: A Brief History of the Twenty-First Century,* "we are now in the process of connecting all of the knowledge pools in the world together" (Friedman, 2005). There's no doubt that the ability of our teachers and students to use that knowledge effectively is of the highest importance.

The second trend is that, more and more, the creation of that content is collaborative. Just about every major software package on the market these days has collaborative tools built in; witness the "Shared Workspace" features of Microsoft Office software that allow teams of people to share and develop documents, presentations, and spreadsheets, to name a few. Or, Google Docs, where you can create documents, spreadsheets, and even presentations with others; publish them easily; and archive them online. Almost every "Web 2.0" tool that comes out these days (and there are thousands of them) makes it easy to connect and create with others. And the open-source development of operating systems such as Linux or browsers like Mozilla's Foxfire is setting a model for collaboration that more and more businesses and even schools are tapping into.

When today's students enter their post-education professional lives, odds are pretty good that they will be asked to work with others from around the globe collaboratively to create content for diverse and wide-ranging audiences. Odds are also pretty good that they are going to need to read and write effectively in linked environments as they locate, analyze, remix, and share the best, most relevant content online for their own learning. Compare that to an educational system that, by and large, asks those same students to work independently on paper for a very narrow audience (usually the teacher who gives the grade), and the disconnect becomes painfully clear.

Right now, teachers are employing Weblogs and wikis and the like in ways that are transforming the curriculum and are allowing learning to continue long after the class ends. They are tapping into the potential of a World Wide Web that is a conversation, not a lecture, where knowledge is shaped and acquired through a social process, and where ideas are presented as a starting point for dialogue, not an ending point (Siemens, 2005). In case after case, the walls of the classroom are literally made irrelevant by the creation of communities of learners that span oceans, races, genders, and generations.

NEW LITERACIES

In the age of the Read/Write Web, the explosion of information and online technologies demands a more complex definition of what it means to be literate. For more than a hundred years we have defined being literate as being able to read and to write. And although those core abilities are still central to learning, they are no longer enough to ensure understanding.

First, due in large measure to the ease with which people can now publish to the Internet, consumers of Web content need to be editors as well as readers. Print sources have always carried with them the assumption that the content included had been reviewed or checked before being published. Books, newspapers, and magazines all have editors whose job it is to make sure the information is verifiably accurate. But today, anyone with an Internet connection can now publish without any prior review. Although this is good in terms of creating a wider body of knowledge to draw from, it obviously requires that we teach our students to become more active consumers of that information rather than passively accepting it as legitimate. Editing, then, means being a critical reader and viewer, not simply accepting what is presented.

Second, to truly take advantage of the power of the Read/Write Web, we must be literate in the ways of publishing. In many ways, we now truly have a free press that the framers of the Constitution envisioned, where everyone can have a voice. We must then teach and model the ways in which ideas and products can be brought online.

Third, we need to know how to manage the information that we consume. Our students will be required to collect, store, and retrieve relevant information throughout their lives, and we need to give them the skills to do so effectively and efficiently.

But most importantly, we must do all of this work with the intent to connect to other people who share our passion. We must begin to understand the nuances of learning in online, virtual spaces with others—not simply to trade stories or reflections nor to simply create content together but to change the world. All around us, there is evidence of that potential, from the uprisings in Iran to the green schools movement to our ability to provide microloans to bush farmers in Sudan. In our networks, we can do good work.

All of these skills support the important, overarching goal of developing students who can flourish in the networked personal learning spaces that they will inhabit the rest of their lives. If we fail to graduate students who are not able to create, sustain, and participate in these networks in safe, ethical, and effective ways, we've done them a disservice.

THE BIG SHIFTS

So, the classroom of the Read/Write Web is one of seamless transfer of information; of collaborative, individualized learning; and of active participation by all members of the class. It is marked by the continuous process of creating and sharing content with wide audiences. In many ways, these technologies are demanding that we reexamine the way we think about content and curriculum, and they are nurturing new, important shifts in how best to teach students.

Big Shift 1: Open Content

It used to be that schools and teachers "owned" the content they taught in their classrooms. Most curriculum was taught from a textbook with a few added resources thrown in. Perhaps there was a filmstrip (remember those?) or a video that added to the discussion. Outside of what schools provided, however, students had limited access to additional information about the subjects they were studying. There were newspapers and magazines, and there were books in the school and public libraries, but all of these resources required more time and effort than the average student wanted to expend.

Today, however, that information is as far away as a Google search or Wikipedia, and the breadth and depth of content are staggering. The information students can access is more current as well, rendering many textbooks passé. In fact, many teachers and students have begun writing their own textbooks online using the collaborative spaces now available to them, cobbling together links and annotated reading lists that future classes can build on as well.

More and more, the "code" to teaching and learning that schools once held dear is disappearing, and is being replaced by open-source-type classrooms in which everyone contributes to the curriculum. This openness leads to the next Big Shift.

Big Shift 2: Many, Many Teachers and 24/7 Learning

As our access to content increases, so does our access to other teachers. Many other teachers, in fact. The Read/Write Web allows us to connect to other science, or English, or social studies teachers. But, in addition to this, we can now also find biochemists, scholars of Faulkner, and Civil War reenactors to bring into the classroom. Teachers who harness the potential of these tools are tapping into the knowledge of primary sources such as authors and historians and researchers. And the asynchronous nature of these tools—the ability to interact with content when it's most convenient to do so—means that learning can take place anytime we're ready for it.

As I've said, in my eight years as a blogger I have found hundreds if not thousands of teachers—people who through their willingness to share their ideas and experiences have informed my practice and my thinking. The rich diversity of cultures, geography, and professional expertise that these sources provide has dramatically broadened my understanding of my own teaching and of education in general. Without question, it has been the most extensive and effective learning experience of my life.

But unlike the traditional student–teacher relationship, the student no longer just consumes the content provided by the teacher. Through my Weblog, I am able to be a part of the conversation and, in turn, perhaps teach other teachers through my reflections and ideas. This creates an opportunity for Big Shift 3.

Big Shift 3: The Social, Collaborative Construction of Meaningful Knowledge

For generations, the typical expectation of our students has been that they work independently ("do your own work") and produce that work or content for a limited audience—usually just the teacher giving the grade and perhaps the other students in the class. The work, once it was finished, was exactly that—finished. Think of how few opportunities there were for anyone outside the classroom walls to "read" those efforts, whether they were essays or experiments or projects or performances. Think of how much of student work today simply ends up in the recycling bin at the end of the year.

Today, however, the Read/Write Web makes it easy for students to produce work in truly collaborative ways for large audiences. That work can have real purpose and real meaning for the audience that reads and consumes it. Information created and published in this way takes on a new social context that requires us to change the way we think about what we ask our students to produce, not as something to be "finished" but as something to be added to and refined by those outside the classroom who may interact with it.

So, this idea that we can continue to interact with our ideas in collaborative ways leads to the next Big Shift.

Big Shift 4: Teaching Is Conversation, Not Lecture

By publishing content to a wide audience, we say "these are my ideas, my understandings of the world at this moment." That in itself is empowering, and with that comes an expectation that our voices will be heard. On their own, our students are learning that their voices matter, that people are listening and responding, and that their ideas count. To not embrace those feelings by continuing to look at curriculum-as-lecture is to fight against a tide that we will not be able to keep back.

As George Siemens says, "Ideas are presented as the starting point for dialogue, not the ending point" (Siemens, 2002). That is the new expectation of the Read/Write Web. To remain relevant, educators are going to have to respond accordingly. By inviting students to become active participants in the design of their own learning, we teach them how to be active participants in their lives and future careers.

This shift from lecture to conversation requires the next Big Shift.

Big Shift 5: Know "Where" Learning

In the Read/Write Web classroom, it's not as essential to know what the answer is as it is to know where to find it. In the past, when information was not as accessible, it was important to memorize facts and formulas. Today, however, factual answers are only a few clicks away. Or, just send a text message with what you need to know, for example, "define inculcate," to 46645 (which spells "GOOGL"), and your phone will ring you back with an answer in seconds.

Knowing "where" learning also means knowing where to find those good teachers mentioned above. As we move away from textbooks and more "closed" sources of information, we need to be able to create our own texts from many different content providers such as Weblogs, wikis, Web sites, discussion groups, and more. So teachers and students have to understand and be able to employ the many different ways to find information on the Web.

And, obviously, it's not enough simply to find these sources. We must be able to identify which of the sources we do find are worthy of our attention. To do so, we need to accept the next Big Shift.

Big Shift 6: Readers Are No Longer Just Readers

In an era of textbooks and printed resources, we could be pretty sure that the content we consumed had been checked and edited before being published. Reading, for all intents, was a fairly passive experience. Today, however, readers cannot assume that someone else has reviewed what they are reading with an eye toward truth and accuracy. The Web is now a printing press for the masses, and so readers themselves must learn to be critical consumers of the information they consider. They must be editors with all of the information literacy skills they need to discern good information from bad.

And now, given the opportunity to converse and interact with the sources they find, readers must also be writers. We must be able to engage those sources in debate and discussion as one way of assessing their worth.

In all of these ways, reading is becoming a more active undertaking, no longer neatly compartmentalized in books and handouts. There is valuable knowledge to be found in thousands, maybe millions of places, which leads us to Big Shift 7.

Big Shift 7: The Web as Notebook (or Portfolio)

As the Web becomes more and more of a source of content for our teaching and learning, it also renders paper less and less effective as a way to capture the information we find relevant. Hence the Read/Write Web. Weblogs and wikis and the like were born out of the need to save and organize the digital ideas we find interesting so that we can annotate them with our own interpretations and easily return to them when we need to.

And not only can we collect links and text in our Web notebooks, we can include audio, video, photography, and more. In fact, many educators see the Web as the perfect home for electronic learner portfolios that can be shared easily with audiences of peers and mentors. To make that happen, we have to accept Big Shift 8.

Big Shift 8: Writing Is No Longer Limited to Text

As we move away from plain text on the page, we move toward a totally new definition of what it means to write. Certainly, in the short term at least, it remains crucially important to be able to express oneself in writing using words. But it is hard to deny that more and more we have become a multimedia society, relying heavily on television to communicate the important ideas of our culture. According to a 2009 study, only about half of Americans over 13 read a book last year (tinyurl.com/12zaxv).

But today, the technologies of the Read/Write Web allow us to write in many different genres. We can write in audio and video, in music, in digital photographs, and even in code such as JavaScript, and we can publish all of it easily for extended audiences. As blogger Alan Levine and others say, we can combine many of these forms of writing into a process of "Rip, Mix, and Learn," taking a piece of content here and another piece there, combining it to produce powerful text and nontext messages and interpretations (Levine, 2004).

These genres of writing expand the ways in which we can prove our knowledge and lead us to the next Big Shift.

Big Shift 9: Mastery Is the Product, Not the Test

The Age of the Read/Write Web is an age not only of participation but also of production. Think about the limited ways in which we could show mastery in the "old" days. For the vast majority, mastery was exhibited by passing the test. When you think about it, schools are one of the very few places where someone is said to have "mastered" a subject by getting 70 percent of the test correct. And most of the tests were not based on what you could do with the information. Would you feel safe in a world where kids were awarded drivers licenses by just passing the written test? I didn't think so.

Today, however, students can display mastery in countless ways that involve the creation of digital content for large audiences. Even more traditional forms of showing mastery through performance or putting together projects can now be easily published to the Web in a variety of ways. More and more, the concept of a cheap, accessible, electronic online portfolio is coming to fruition. Leading to the next Big Shift.

Big Shift 10: Contribution, Not Completion, as the Ultimate Goal

All of these technologies allow students and teachers to contribute their own ideas and work to the larger body of knowledge that is the Web. Instead of simply handing in countless assignments to teachers to be read, graded, handed back, and most likely thrown away, we can now offer our students a totally new way of looking at the work they do. It's not meant for the teacher or the class or even the school. It's meant for the world—literally. It's not meant to be discarded or stored in a folder somewhere; it's meant to be added to the conversation and potentially used to teach others.

Obviously, these changes create all sorts of challenges for educators, challenges to the educational system as a whole, and challenges to the traditional roles of teachers in the classroom. First, the educational system itself will be under pressure to respond to the ability of students to learn 24/7 from a variety of sources. The neatly organized four- or eight-period day, 180-day school year may no longer be the most effective structure to teach students in a world filled with easy access to information. The vertical model of a teacher disseminating information and knowledge to students may not be very effective in an environment in which learning is a much more horizontal or collaborative undertaking. But those types of systemic changes will be a long time in coming.

More important will be the response of classroom teachers, for the classroom of the Read/Write Web will in many ways require a redefinition of what it means to teach.

First, teachers will have to start to see themselves as *connectors,* not only of content, but of people. Once again, the access to much greater amounts and more timely information means that it will be imperative for educators to model strategies not only to find worthwhile and relevant content, but to use primary sources in the classroom. We can invite people from around the world to engage in discussions and even content creation with our students, and our teachers must be willing and able to find and use these sources effectively.

Second, teachers must become *content creators* as well. To teach these technologies effectively, educators must learn to use them effectively. They need to become bloggers and podcasters, to use wikis and the other social tools at their disposal. They need, in short, to know how to build and sustain their own personal learning networks. Just like anyone else trying to learn a new language, educators must practice the words, or, in this case, the tools. Chris Dede of the Graduate School of Education at Harvard says, "Teachers who use interactive media professionally will find they rapidly develop learning styles and strengths similar to those of their students" (as quoted in Thatcher, 2005). And they might even come to enjoy it.

Connecting and contributing are not enough, however. Teachers also need to become true *collaborators.* And not just with each other, but with their students as well. For all of the reasons I've previously cited, teachers must begin to see themselves more as learners alongside their students. The "New 'Net" allows us to tap into the creativity and knowledge of thousands if not millions of teachers and students, and we have to be willing to learn together—both in the classroom and online—to effectively give our students the most relevant experience we can. We can't pretend to know everything any more, and we can't be effective if we don't tap into the work of others who are willing to contribute their ideas and content as well.

Fourth, teachers need to think of themselves more as *coaches* who model the skills that students need to be successful and motivate them to strive for excellence. Ultimately, players on the field take responsibility for their own performance, and they learn through practice and reflection. That needs to be true of students now as well. We teach students the skills of the Read/Write Web and motivate them to seek their own truths and their own learning.

Finally, teachers who use the tools of the Read/Write Web need to be *change agents*. The ideas will not be easily embraced or readily supported at first because of the transparency they create. So teachers need to find ways to use these tools to move away from the more traditional paradigms of instruction on their own terms in their own ways and recruit others to follow suit.

JUST THE BEGINNING

We are still at the beginning of a radically different relationship with the Internet, one that has long-standing implications for educators and students. The coming years will be marked by a flood of new innovations and ideas in teaching, most born from the idea that we can now publish and interact in ways never before possible. In reality, we now have a Read/Reflect/Write/Participate Web, one that will continue to evolve and grow in ways not yet thought of, spurred by the efforts of creative teachers who recognize the potential to improve student learning.

If you have come this far, I'm hoping you have a new box of tools and techniques to take full advantage of the opportunities this new Internet presents. Here is where the real learning,

Epilogue

The Classroom of the Read/Write Web

English teacher Tom McHale sets down his cup of coffee and boots up the computer at his classroom desk. It's 6:50 a.m., and he has about 45 minutes before his sleepy journalism students will begin filing into his classroom. He logs in and opens up his personal Weblog on the school intranet. There, he does a quick scan of the *New York Times* headlines that are displayed on his homepage and clicks on one of the links to read a story about war reporting that he thinks his student journalists might be interested in. Using his Diigo toolbar, he highlights the lead paragraph and then adds a sticky note annotation asking his students to analyze the effectiveness of the writing. With a quick click, Tom chooses "bookmark" on his toolbar, adds a bit of annotation to the form that comes up, and saves it to his Diigo journalism group. With this one step, he archives the page for future reference and automatically sends the link and his note via RSS to display on his journalism class portal for students to read when they log in.

Next, he scans a compiled list of summaries that links to all the work his students submitted to their Weblogs the night before. Seeing one particularly well-done response, he clicks through to the student's personal site and leaves a positive comment about her submission. (He notices that a couple of his students have already left some positive feedback to the author as well.) He also "Diigos" that site, tagging it to his "Best Practices" list, which will send it to the class homepage as well for students to read and discuss, and to a separate Weblog page he has created to keep track of all of the best examples of student work. It's now 7:00 a.m.

After taking a sip of his coffee, Tom takes a look at his research feeds. He's been asked to keep abreast of the latest news about technology and teaching writing, and this morning he sees his Google search feed has turned up a new version of Zoho Office. He clicks the link, reads about the new version on the site, and then clicks on a different "Diigo" button that uses an account set up for all of his department colleagues to share. When the form comes up, he writes a couple of lines of description about how it might benefit the department, and then saves it in the "Technology" list, which automatically archives it to the tech page of the English Department Weblog. Later that day, all the members of his department will see his link along with any others his colleagues may have added as a part of their daily e-mail update from Diigo. He also decides he wants to create another search feed for the words "journalism" and "Weblogs." With a click on the toolbar, a dialog box appears. He enters his terms, and then clicks on the Feedster.com radio button (one among four choices). He hits OK, and a new feed headline box is added to his portal.

At around 7:05, Tom uses his personal Weblog to upload an assignment on symbolism for his Major American Literature class. When he opens up the document online to check it, he adds it to a different Diigo group under his English login, and it gets sent to a separate Web page set up on the English site for American Literature Best Practices. The rest of the American Lit teachers will get an automatic e-mail later in the day notifying them of his published artifact, which they can use in their own classes. Then, he creates a post for his Lit class portal that has a link to the assignment, and he publishes the post to the class homepage. Automatically, parents who have requested notification will get an e-mail that their son or daughter has homework to do that evening. E-mails also get sent to a couple of counselors who are tracking at-risk students.

At about 7:15, Tom decides to scan the latest school news feed, which aggregates all the new posts from the school Weblogs he is subscribed to. He sees that the basketball team won the county tournament, the new edition of the school paper is online, and the superintendent has posted important information about an upcoming safety drill. He clicks through to read the entire post, and then leaves a comment suggesting a way to alleviate crowding in the hallways during the drill. (He sees a parent also has a suggestion about the timing.) Back at his page, he decides that he doesn't want to scan the soccer team news any longer, so he goes to his subscription page and unchecks the feed. He does notice, however, the "New Feeds" section lists a new "Tech Deals" feed that the tech supervisor has created. Because he's looking for a new home computer, he clicks to subscribe to it.

At 7:25, he checks his audio library and sees that the MP3 interview that two of his students did with the principal has been downloaded to his player. He lifts it out of its cradle and puts it in his briefcase so he can play it on his car stereo during his ride home after school. If it's good, he'll upload it to the school podcast page, where 135-odd subscribers (mostly parents) will automatically receive it so they can hear it and hopefully get most of their questions about the new building project answered.

With just a few minutes left before his first class, Tom opens the personal journal part of his portal and types in a few notes about an idea he had for the lit project his students are completing next week. He files them into the "Literature" subfolder so he can pull up relevant notes all at once if he needs to. Now that his volume of e-mail has been drastically reduced, he scans the few messages in his inbox, takes a last gulp of coffee, and opens his classroom door to the sound of happy students.

References

Alpert, J., & Hajaj, N. (2008, July 25). We knew the Web was big… *The Official Google Blog.* Retrieved October 18, 2009, from http://googleblog.blogspot.com/2008/07/we-knew-web-was-big.html.

Barrett, H. (2004). *Versions of my online portfolios.* Retrieved September 25, 2005, from http://electronicportfolios.org/myportfolio/versions.html.

Bischoff, M. (2005). *Esc from the world! Weblog and podcasts about software and technology by teenage geek Matthew Bischoff.* Retrieved November 7, 2005, from http://matthewbischoff.com/.

Booth, M. (2007, May 1). Grading Wikipedia [Electronic Edition]. *Denver Post.* Retrieved October 20, 2009, from http://www.denverpost.com/search/ci_5786064.

Brooks, S. (2005a, April 18). *iPod in educations.* Retrieved April 18, 2005, from http://www.edugadget.com/2005/04/18/ipod-lessons-for-all-of-us/.

Brooks, S. (2005b, May 7). *Flickr creative commons.* Retrieved September 25, 2005, from http://www.edugadget.com/2005/05/07/flickr-creative-commons/.

Burrell, C. (2007, March 23). From red pen to invisible ink: Assessing student blogs with Diigo groups. *Beyond School.* Retrieved October 23, 2009, from http://beyond-school.org/2007/03/23/from-red-pen-to-invisible-ink-assessing-student-blogs-with-diigo-groups/.

Carvin, A. (2005, February 1). *Tim Berners-Lee: Weaving a semantic web.* Retrieved September 25, 2005, from http://www.digitaldivide.net/articles/view.php?ArticleID=20.

Davis, A. (2005). *The write weblog: Who says elementary students can't blog?* Retrieved September 25, 2005, from http://itc.blogs.com/thewriteweblog/2004/11/who_says_elemen.html.

Downes, S. (2005, July 16). *Stephen's Web: Principles for evaluating Web sites.* Retrieved September 25, 2005, from http://www.downes.ca/cgi-bin/page.cgi?db=post&q=crdate=1121531748&format=full.

Educause Learning Initiative. (2005, May). *7 things you should know about social bookmarking.* Retrieved November 5, 2005, from http://www.educause.edu/ir/library/pdf/ELI7001.pdf.

Eide Neurolearning Blog. (2005, March 2). *Brain of the blogger.* Retrieved September 25, 2005, from http://eideneurolearningblog.blogspot.com/2005/03/brain-of-blogger.html.

FCC Consumer and Governmental Affairs Bureau. (2003, September 17). *Children's Internet Protection Act.* Retrieved September 25, 2005, from http://www.fcc.gov/cgb/consumerfacts/cipa.html.

Fisher, C. (2007, January 30). *Signal vs. noise.* Retrieved October 14, 2009, from http://remoteaccess.typepad.com/remote_access/2007/01/signal_vs_noise.html.

Friedman, T. (2005). *The world is flat: A brief history of the twenty-first century.* New York: Farrar, Strauss and Giroux.

Ganley, B. (2004a, October). *bgblogging: October 2004 archives.* Retrieved September 25, 2005, from http://mt.middlebury.edu/middblogs/ganley/bgblogging/2004_10.html#004423.

Ganley, B. (2004b, November). *bgblogging: November 2004 archives.* Retrieved September 25, 2005, from http://mt.middlebury.edu/middblogs/ganley/bgblogging/2004_11.html#005353.

Gillmor, D. (2005). The Read-Write Web. *We the media.* Retrieved September 25, 2005, from http://www.authorama.com/we-the-media-3.html.

Ginty, D. (2002, September 26). Questions for the author. *The secret life of bees: We're making the reader study guide!* Retrieved October 21, 2009, from http://weblogs.hcrhs.k12.nj.us/bees/discuss/msgReader$217.

Glogowski, K. (2005, May 15). Writing vs. blogging (Part 2). In *Blog of proximal development.* Retrieved September 25, 2005, from http://www.teachandlearn.ca/blog/2005/05/15/writing-vs-blogging-part-2/.

Graham, J. (2004, December 14). Google's library plan "a huge help." *USA Today.* Retrieved September 26, 2005, from http://www.usatoday.com/money/industries/technology/2004–12–14-google-usat_x.htm.

Halavais, A. (2004, August 29). The *Isuzu experiment.* Retrieved September 25, 2005, from http://alex.halavais.net/the-isuzu-experiment/.

Hoffman, T. (2005, June 24). NECC talking points: Blogs as resources. *Ed-tech insider.* Retrieved November 3, 2005, from http://www.eschoolnews.com/eti/2005/06/000877.php.

Hunt, B. (2005). *Bud's blog experiment.* Retrieved November 2, 2005, from http://budtheteacher.typepad.com/bud_the_teacher/.

Ito, M., Horst, H., Bittanti, M., boyd, d., Herr-Stephenson, B., Lange, P.G., et al. (2008). *Summary of findings from the digital youth project.* Retrieved October 22, 2009, from http://digitalyouth.ischool.berkeley.edu/files/report/digitalyouth-WhitePaper.pdf.

Jakes, D. (2005, May 10). *The strength of weak ties: Sandburg meets flickr.* Retrieved September 25, 2005, from http://jakespeak.blogspot.com/2005/05/sandburg-meets-flickr.html.

Jupiter Research. (2007, May 29). *Jupiter Research forecasts 70 percent of US households to have broadband by 2012.* Retrieved October 20, 2009, from http://www.redorbit.com/news/technology/949114/jupiterresearch_forecasts_70_percent_of_us_households_to_have_broadband/index.html.

Kidd, S. M. (2002). *The secret life of bees.* New York: Penguin.

Keller, J. (2009, July 9). Study explores whether the Internet makes students better writers. *The Chronicle of Higher Education.* Retrieved October 23, 2009, from http://chronicle.com/article/Studies-Explore-Whether-the/44476/.

Koman, R. (2005, January 8). Are blogs the new journalism? *O'Reilly developer Weblogs.* Retrieved September 25, 2005, from http://www.oreillynet.com/digitalmedia/blog/2005/01/are_blogs_the_new_journalism.html.

Kuropatwa, D. (2005, March 20). *Pre-Cal 40S: HERE!! HERE!!* Retrieved September 25, 2005, from http://pc40s.blogspot.com/2005/03/here-here.html.

Lardinois, F. (2009, April 16). Ning now hosts over 1 million social networks. *ReadWriteWeb*. Retrieved October 18, 2009, from http://www.readwriteweb.com/archives/ning_now_hosts_1_million_social_networks.php#more.

Lenhart, A., Fallows, D., & Horrigan, J. (2004, February 29). Online activities & pursuits. *Pew Internet & American Life Project*. Retrieved October 26, 2000, from http://www.pewtrusts.org/our_work_detail.aspx?id=50

Lenhart, A., Madden, M., Macgill, A.R., & Smith, A. (December 19, 2007). Teen content creators. *Pew Internet and American life project*. Retrieved October 20, 2009, from http://pewresearch.org/pubs/670/teen-content-creators.

Leu, D.J., O'Byrne, W.I., Zawilinski, L., McVerry, J.G., & Everett-Cacopardo, H. (2009) Expanding the new literacies conversation [Electronic version]. *Educational Researcher, 38*(4), 264–269. Retrieved October 9, 2009, from http://www.aera.net/uploadedFiles/Publications/Journals/Educational_Researcher/3804/264-269_05EDR09.pdf.

Levine, A. (2004, September 23). *Rip. Mix. Learn . . . The digital generation, social technologies, and learning.* A presentation for the Training Expo Partners Conference, September 23, 2004. Retrieved November 14, 2005, from http://graphite.mcli.dist.maricopa.edu/emerging/wiki?RipMixLearn.

Moorman, H, (2009). Adventures in Web 2.0: Introducing social networking into my teaching. *Horace 25*(1). Retrieved October 18, 2009, from tinyurl.com/ltbzx2.

National Council of Teachers of English. (2008). *The definition of twenty-first century literacies.* Retrieved October 9, 2009, from http://www.ncte.org/governance/literacies.

National Council of Teachers of English. (2009). *NCTE/IRA standards for the English language arts.* Retrieved October 20, 2009, from http://www.ncte.org/standards.

National Education Technology Plan. (2005). Retrieved September 25, 2005, from http://www.cd.gov/about/offices/list/os/technology/plan/2004/site/edlitedefault.html.

NetDay News. (2005, March 8). *NetDay's 2004 survey results show 58 percent of students have cell phones, 60 percent e-mail or IM adults on a weekly basis.* Retrieved September 25, 2005, from http://www.netday.org/news_2004_survey_results.htm.

Olofson, C. (1999, December). Just the (meaningful) facts. *Fast Company, 30.* Retrieved November 13, 2005, from http://www.fastcompany.com/magazine/30/futurist.html.

Paulina's Club. (2005, May 5). Retrieved on November 3, 2005, from http://itc.blogs.com/paulina/2005/05/our_lives_at_jh.html.

Pell, M. (2007, November 19). *The future of reading.* Retrieved October 9, 2009, from http://myfla.ws/blog/2007/11/19/future-of-reading/.

Perry, D. (2006). The technology of reading and writing in the digital space: Why RSS is crucial for a blogging classroom. *Blogs for Learning.* Retrieved October, 14, 2009, from http://blogsforlearning.msu.edu/articles/view.php?id=6.

Prensky, M. (2001). *Digital natives, digital immigrants.* Retrieved September 25, 2005, from http://www.marcprensky.com/writing/Prensky%20%20Digital%20Natives,%20Digital%20Immigrants%20-%20Part1.pdf.

Prensky, M. (2004). *The emerging online life of the digital native: What they do differently because of technology, and how they do it.* Retrieved December 30,

2004, from http://www.marcprensky.com/writing/Prensky-The_Emerging_Online_Life_of_the_Digital_Native-03.pdf.

Rheingold, H. (2004, November 4). *M-learning 4 generation txt?* Retrieved September 25, 2005, from http://www.thefeaturearchives.com/101157.html.

Rheingold, H. (2007, October 2). *Vision of the future.* Retrieved October 8, 2009, from http://www.educationau.edu.au/jahia/webdav/site/myjahiasite/shared/seminars/Rheingold_Melbourne_Speech.pdf.

Rushkoff, D. (2004, October, 10). *Renaissance prospects.* Retrieved September 25, 2005, from http://www.itconversations.com/shows/detai1243.html.

Shirkey, C. (2008) *Here comes everybody: The power of organizing without organizations.* New York: Penguin.

Siemens, G. (2002, December 1). The art of blogging. *elearnspace: Everything elearning.* Retrieved September 26, 2005, from http://www.elearnspace.org/Articles/blogging_part_1.htm.

Smith, J. (2009, July 2). Facebook now growing by over 700,000 users a day, and new engagement stats. *Inside Facebook.* Retrieved October 23, 2009, from http://www.insidefacebook.com/2009/07/02/facebook-now-growing-by-over-700000-users-a-day-updated-engagement-stats/.

Smith, K. (2004, March 30). *CCCC waves and ripples.* Retrieved September 25, 2005, from http://www.mchron.net/site/edublog_comments.php?id=P2636_0_13_0.

Thatcher, M. (2005, March 15). The back page: Q & A with Chris Dede. *School CEO: The Newsletter for K–12 Technology Leaders.* Retrieved November 14, 2005, from http://www.techlearning.com/story/showArticle.jhtml?articleID=60407857.

Valenza, J. (2009, March 12). If I had my way: More unquiet libraries. *Neverendingsearch.* Retrieved October 20, 2009, from http://www.schoollibraryjournal.com/blog/1340000334/post/1090041909.html.

Wales, J. (2004). Jimmy Wales. *Wikiquote.* Retrieved November 3, 2005, from http://en.wikiquote.org/wiki/Jimmy_Wales.

Wojewodzki, R. (2009, May 14). Best practices in a Twitter-enhanced classroom. *Teach Paperless.* Retrieved October 23, 2009, from http://teachpaperless.blogspot.com/2009/05/best-practices-in-twitter-enhanced-high.html.

Index

CORWIN

A SAGE Company

The Corwin logo—a raven striding across an open book—represents the union of courage and learning. Corwin is committed to improving education for all learners by publishing books and other professional development resources for those serving the field of PreK–12 education. By providing practical, hands-on materials, Corwin continues to carry out the promise of its motto: **"Helping Educators Do Their Work Better."**